QUICK & EASY, PROVEN RECIPES

Eat Vegan

Publisher & Creative Director: Nick Wells
Senior Project Editor: Catherine Taylor
Editorial Assistant: Taylor Bentley
Contributing Author: Saskia Fraser
Art Director: Mike Spender
Layout Design: Jane Ashley
Digital Design & Production: Chris Herbert

Special thanks to Frances Bodiam.

Flame Tree Publishing
6 Melbray Mews, Fulham,
London SW6 3NS
United Kingdom
www.flametreepublishing.com

This edition first published 2018

18 20 22 21 19
1 3 5 7 9 10 8 6 4 2

ISBN: 978-1-78755-234-0

Publisher's Note: Due to the closely related nature of vegan and vegetarian food,
some of the recipes featured in this book are also included in *Quick & Easy Proven Recipes: Vegetarian*.

A copy of the CIP data for this book is available from the British Library.

Printed in China

All images © Flame Tree Publishing Ltd, except for the following which are © StockFood and the following: 9t Paul, Michael; 43 Koene, Robbert; 45 Paul, Michael; 47 Hendey, Magdalena; 83 Gräfe & Unzer Verlag / Schardt, Wolfgang; 93 Short, Jonathan; 133 Gräfe & Unzer Verlag / Zanin, Melanie; 145 Garlick, Ian; 155 Eising Studio - Food Photo & Video; 175 Parissi, Lucy; 225 Studio Lipov; 229 Hendey, Magdalena; 249 Morgans, Gareth.Courtesy Shutterstock.com and the following: 4 alexpro9500; 6br yesyesterday; 8 Oleksandra Naumenko; 9b Oko Laa; 10t symbiot; 10b Nemanja Novakovic; 12 ocphoto; 14 Family Business; 15 Degtiarova Viktoriia; 16 Jurga Jot; 17 Natasha Breen; 18 fotolotos; 20 Peangdao; 21 baibaz; 22 thefoodphotographer; 23 yingko; 24 Kerdkanno; 25 Leszek Glasner; 26 Yulia Grigoryeva; 28 JRP Studio; 30 zi3000; 31b Africa Studio; 35 Natasha Breen; 37 Africa Studio; 39 AS Food studio; 41 tacar; 65 Maria Komar; 111 bonchan; 149 Anna_Pustynnikova; 159 Joshua Resnick; 161 Elena Veselova; 163 Ievgeniia Maslovska; 167 Razmarinka; 177 Lilyana Vynogradova; 203 Ulyana Khorunzha; 205 Soumitra Pendse; 223 Tatiana Vorona; 227 Family Business; 233 thefoodphotographer; 239 Yulia Davidovich; 243 Edith Frincu; 253 Mshev; 11 Foxys Forest Manufacture; 13 natalia bulatova; 27 K2 PhotoStudio; 29 Ekaterina Kondratova; 49 Maria Shumova; 51 Liliya Kandrashevich; 53 AlenaKogotkova; 55 Anna Kurzaeva; 57 Jayme Burrows; 59 Kiian Oksana; 63 Brent Hofacker; 69 Oleg B-art; 77 VICUSCHKA; 89 natalia bulatova; 95 Virginia Garcia; 105 marco mayer; 137 marco mayer; 251 Kati Molin.

QUICK & EASY, PROVEN RECIPES

Eat Vegan

General Editor: Gina Steer

FLAME TREE
PUBLISHING

Contents

Introducing
Veganism

The chapters ahead are packed with an abundance of delicious and flavoursome vegan recipes to satisfy every palate. However, before you jump right in, take a moment to discover more about the history and benefits of veganism, and dispel some common misconceptions. You'll also find indispensable advice about how to transition to a vegan lifestyle while still getting all the nutrients you need.

What Does it Mean to Be Vegan?

Veganism has seen a huge surge in popularity since the 1970s. It is a fuller expression of vegetarianism, and is an ethical lifestyle choice. Someone who takes on the mantle of 'vegan' aims to ensure no animals are harmed by their choices.

A Brief History of Veganism

There is evidence of the deliberate avoidance of animal products dating back over 2000 years. Around 500 BC, Pythagoras was promoting a benevolence among all species and eating in accordance with his values. About the same time, Buddha was teaching vegetarian principles – having compassion for the animals of our planet, and therefore not eating them – to his followers.

The Vegan Movement

Modern day veganism began as a more developed version of vegetarianism in 1944, when Donald Watson decided that 'vegetarian' did not adequately describe his diet and lifestyle choices and, along with a group of six other non-dairy vegetarians, coined the term 'vegan'.

Today

Nowadays, many people are choosing veganism for health reasons as well as reasons of conscience. Many famous actors, models and pop stars are choosing and promoting veganism, and it has also become a fashionable lifestyle choice. World Vegan Day is 1 November, when veganism is celebrated and championed.

Veganism Defined

Veganism in its broadest sense is the choice to live a cruelty-free lifestyle. For some, this only applies to food choices. For others, it extends to their clothes, cosmetics, household products and anything else that may have caused harm to an animal. The first official definition of veganism was created in 1949 as 'The principle of the emancipation of animals from exploitation by man'. After a few more clarifications over the years, the Vegan Society's official definition of veganism is now: 'A philosophy and way of living which seeks to exclude – as far as is possible and practicable – all forms of exploitation of, and cruelty to, animals for food, clothing or any other purpose; and by extension, promotes the development and use of animal-free alternatives for the benefit of humans, animals and the environment. In dietary terms it denotes the practice of dispensing with all products derived wholly or partly from animals.'

What Vegans Eat

Being a vegan means that you don't eat animal products: no meat; no fish; no eggs; no dairy products, such as cheese, milk, yogurt, whey or butter; no bee products, such as honey, bee pollen or propolis; no gelatine, or anything else that comes from, is made by or includes an animal.

What does it mean to be Vegan?

What Vegans Wear

If you choose to take the vegan principles further into your life, this will mean no leather shoes, belts or clothing; no woollen clothes or accessories; and no accessories made from shells, pearls or feathers, or anything else that comes from, is made by or includes an animal.

Cosmetics

By fully embracing a vegan lifestyle you choose to be conscious of and conscientious about everything you use in your life. The vast majority of ingredients in beauty and bathroom products are tested on animals. Check that cosmetics, shampoos, conditioners, moisturizers, cleansers, toners and hair dyes are marked 'cruelty-free' before you buy them.

Household Products

Washing up liquid, laundry detergent, fabric conditioner, bleach, household cleaners, air fresheners and upholstery cleaners are another area where animal testing is widely used. Glues and wax often contain animal products. Do your research to find out which brands are not tested on animals and look for the vegan mark.

Modern Versus Traditional Veganism

Veganism used to be seen as very extreme and limiting, with a 'holier-than-though' image. However, over the last decade many inspiring and creative vegans have turned this image around. Veganism has now filtered into top restaurants and is being made more popular by celebrities and high-profile chefs. Plant-based is the new cool!

Dispelling the Myths about Veganism

There are many myths and untruths that you will have heard regarding veganism. Read on and you will see how little weight – if any – these statements carry:

'Vegan Food is Bland & Boring'

Just like any other kind of food, vegan food can be boring – but it can also be delicious. Vegan flavours are rich, deep, fresh, light, spicy, complex, simple and sophisticated, and ingredients can be local, international or exotic. Whatever your preferences, there is a world of exciting vegan recipes to explore.

Get Ready for a Taste Sensation!

Vegan recipes used to have a reputation for being 'brown bread and beans', but today there is worldwide inspiration and flavours are at your fingertips. Whether you love hearty stews, Thai curries, Italian-inspired salads or Mexican food, there is plenty to get excited about.

Vegan Ingredients

Vegan ingredients are plentiful and easy to find everywhere. With a few simple elements, you can easily make something in minutes that tastes amazing. And, if you want to spend time in the kitchen, you can create serious comfort food or a sophisticated dinner party dish worthy of royalty.

Cutting Out Meat & Cheese

If you are new to being vegan, you may wonder how exciting food can be without meat, fish, eggs and cheese. Let me assure you, it won't be long before you don't miss the taste of animal ingredients at all. Plus, vegan cheese and meat substitutes are now readily available.

'Veganism is Not Healthy for You'

There is a myth that getting the right nutrition is not possible on a vegan diet. Of course, it is possible to be an unhealthy vegan, as it is to be an unhealthy meat-eater, but there are numerous studies showing that a flesh-free diet can in fact be better for you.

Where to Get Your Nutrition

As a healthy vegan it's important to know where to get certain nutrients on a plant-based diet. Meat is a major source of iron, while eggs and dairy are the standard dietary source of B12. Take a closer look at nutrition in the section on transitioning to a vegan lifestyle.

Junk Veganism

It is very easy to be a 'junk vegan'. Many unhealthy processed, pre-packaged and fast food options are available. An uninformed vegan can easily end up living off bread, pasta, fries and vegan cheese, while being frustrated that they have pimples and that they are putting on weight.

Real Food Veganism

Being a real-food vegan means that you take care of yourself, as well as the animals on the planet, by eating whole food ingredients that nourish, energize and replenish you. It means using lots of fresh veggies and fruit as well as the plethora of other plant-based ingredients that are available.

'Being Vegan is Time-consuming & Difficult'

In transitioning to a vegan diet, many people take longer than they would like to because they think it is time-consuming and difficult. While it's true that you need to learn new ways of cooking and be more mindful when eating out or eating with friends, it can also simplify life.

Vegan Recipes

Vegan recipes can be super easy without compromising on flavour. You can whizz up a salad, soup or sandwich in minutes. Cruelty-free recipes are no more difficult or time-consuming than any other kind of recipes, and are a great opportunity to expand your recipe repertoire while loving the planet.

Eating with Friends & Family

Have fun! Impress your friends and family with the kinds of recipes that are possible without using animal products. Have vegan dinner parties or relaxed weekend lunches as a way of introducing them to the deliciousness of plant-based eating. Keep them in their comfort zone by trying recipes that look like traditional recipes, but without the animal products.

Eating Out

Eating out as a vegan is becoming a lot easier. Research which restaurants offer vegan dishes, as well as seeking out dedicated vegan locations. If you find yourself at a place without vegan options, ask for something special. Not all chefs understand what is and isn't vegan, so be explicit.

'Veganism is About Denial'

There is no need to worry about what you are giving up by becoming vegan. There are many talented people in the vegan world, pushing the boundaries of what is possible on a plant-based diet. With recipes like egg- and dairy-free pancakes (*see* pages 54 and 154), vegan cheesecakes (*see* pages 226 and 242) and spaghetti with meatless balls (*see* page 178), who needs denial?

Vegan Dairy Substitutes

People often think they will miss dairy products when they go vegan. Luckily, there are delicious, cruelty-free alternatives that make letting go of dairy easy. There are plenty of recipes for fresh, plant-based milks, cheeses and yogurt, as well as pre-packaged options for when you want 'melty' cheese or grab-and-go milk or yogurt.

Vegan Desserts

If you love rich and creamy desserts, fear not! Vegan desserts are amazing and much better for your health than dairy-filled ones. Vegan recipes work magic with coconut cream, frozen bananas and even avocados. You will never miss your old favourites. Love custard? Love ice cream? You are in for a vegan treat!

Vegan Baking

Traditional baking calls for copious amounts of eggs, butter and cream. So how does vegan baking work? Cruelty-free baking uses plant-based alternatives and slightly different techniques to create the same effects as traditional baking –whether it's making sure ovens are properly heated, mixing in just the right way or using leavening agents like bicarbonate of soda or egg-replacers such as flax gels and 'aquafaba' (the water from a can of chickpeas!). Divine cakes, biscuits, baked desserts and even meringues are possible without causing any harm to animals.

The Case for Going Vegan

P eople usually decide to go vegan for ethical reasons – for the sake of animal welfare or out of concern for the environment – but there are other benefits to choosing veganism, from health-related to financial.

Ethics & Environment

Caring for our fellow animals and the planet, the desire to have no part in the harming of other sentient beings, is a noble and beautiful cause. It's not always an easy decision, but it is an important one.

The Dairy Industry

The mechanized, mass-production dairy industry uses a cruel method of harvesting milk, predominantly from cows, but also from sheep and goats. These gentle mammals produce milk when they give birth, as humans do. The dairy cycle begins with impregnation through artificial insemination. Within 24 hours of being born, calves are removed from their mothers, causing trauma to both. The mother's milk supply is artificially maintained through machine milking, causing more suffering and, often, mastitis infections. One year later, the cycle begins again. A dairy cow is usually considered spent after 7–8 years, instead of their natural 25-year life expectancy, at which point they are slaughtered.

The Fish & Seafood Industry

Overfishing is bringing many species to the brink of extinction, while mercury levels are dangerously high in larger fish. Incidental capture in fishing nets is the single largest threat to most species of turtles, while an estimated 300,000 small whales, dolphins and porpoises also die this way every year.

The Meat Industry

As well as being cruel, the meat industry is one of the leading causes of deforestation and global warming, due to the feeding of and waste emissions created by billions of farmed animals. Factory farming of animals is incredibly inhumane. They are treated as production units rather than sentient beings, with little or no space to move; feed that contains growth hormones and antibiotics; and short lifespans focused specifically on fattening for slaughter. Even 'free-range' and 'organic' farming methods can be suspect and are not always cruelty-free.

The Egg Industry

From hatching to slaughter, commercial laying hens are mutilated, confined and deprived of their naturally social and curious ways. Even free-range hens may be kept in crowded dark barns at times, and it is common practice to trim the beaks of battery and free-range hens. These laying hens are considered spent after only 12–18 months and sent to slaughter. Then there is the slaughter every year of over 100 million newborn male chicks – no good for the egg industry and the wrong breed for meat.

The Bee Industry

Bees and other pollinators are an essential part of our survival. They pollinate crops to feed us and wild plants to keep the diversity and richness of the planet's flora alive. Consuming bee products in the form of honey, bee pollen, royal jelly, propolis and beeswax exploits these beautiful and important insects.

Health, Energy & Wellbeing

Eating a vegan diet often gives people a sense of wellbeing they have not experienced for many years. Eating animal products can be hard on the digestion, as well as acidifying to the body.

When you cut these out and eat more whole foods, a natural balance is often restored.

Food Intolerances

Many people have food intolerances they aren't aware of until they cut certain foods out. One of the most common intolerances is to dairy products. Many of us do not produce the enzyme needed to digest dairy, causing mild to severe conditions, including:

- Acne and eczema
- Nausea and/or vomiting
- Diarrhoea and/or constipation
- Digestive discomfort
- Runny nose and/or nasal congestion
- Tight chest and difficulty breathing
- Migraines
- Colic in babies

Eggs are another food source that people can be intolerant to, with similar symptoms to those of dairy intolerance. When people become vegan, they often notice a marked improvement in their health.

Weight Loss

Eating a real-food vegan diet can be a healthy way to achieve long-term weight loss. Eating more whole foods means you naturally eat fewer toxic weight-gain foods. A vegan diet is high in fibre, which fills you up and helps with healthy digestion. If you would like to lose weight on a vegan diet, eat a high proportion of fresh vegetables. Stay away from white potatoes, rice and pasta, and eat low-carb vegetables, such as sweet potatoes and plantains instead. Reduce your intake of processed and sweet foods to a minimum and drink plenty of fresh juice and water.

Vegan Savings

Without the need to buy expensive meat, cheese and fish, having a cruelty-free diet is not just good for the planet, it is good for your wallet too. Real-food veganism is a cost-efficient way to eat, as well as being good for you. Pre-packaged and processed vegan foods (such as cheese and meat substitutes) aren't cheap, but they tend to be used more as a treat rather than as a staple part of a vegan diet. So, for health and savings, keep your ingredients fresh and real the majority of the time.

A New Passion

Being vegan offers new and exciting avenues for keen cooks. Turning your compassion for the planet into passion in the kitchen will keep you excited and inspired. There are so many new ways of cooking that become available when you stop relying on standard, animal-based ingredients. Discover what's possible by searching on the internet, buying vegan recipe books, finding local vegan groups and visiting vegan restaurants. Many famous cooks and chefs who used to rely heavily on animal products are now experimenting with plant-based recipes. Your new passion is in fashion!

Humanity

Humans are animals, yet this fact is often lost on us. If being vegan is about caring for animals, about not exploiting the animal world, that also includes our own species. Taking care of ourselves and of each other is just as important as taking care of the rest of the animal kingdom. Eat healthily, keep hydrated, get enough sleep and show yourself and your fellow humans kindness and compassion. Try not to preach or judge, and you will be an inspirational vegan. When we take care of ourselves physically and emotionally, we have more love to give every living thing.

Making the Transition

T ransitioning to a vegan lifestyle can be a gradual, immediate or partial process. Cutting out animal products is a big adjustment for your body and inevitably leads to potential cravings. Whichever way you make the switch, there are a few points to consider that will make the transition easier, both physically and emotionally.

Gradual Transition

A gradual transition is when you cut one ingredient or animal product out at a time, repeating this over a number of weeks or months until the transition to a vegan diet is complete. The benefits include reducing potentially uncomfortable detoxification symptoms and cravings.

Immediate Transition

An immediate transition is when you exclude animal products all at once. This is the most common way to make the switch – for many, the moral imperative, once acknowledged, becomes very important to fulfil straight away.

A Partial Versus Full Transition

Some vegans feel that the only way to embrace the vegan lifestyle is fully, while others choose to embrace a cruelty-free diet without transitioning their whole lives. Vegan shoes, cosmetics and household products can be expensive and hard to find; you may choose to forego this aspect of the vegan lifestyle.

Nutrition

𝓔

People often have concerns about how healthy being vegan is. If you don't have these concerns yourself, family and friends may do. While it is possible to be an unhealthy vegan, it is also possible to be vibrantly healthy on a plant-based diet. There are a few common, vegan-related nutritional misconceptions, the main ones being that calcium can only be obtained through dairy products and that meat, fish, eggs and dairy are the only sources of protein. While this is untrue, there are a few key nutrients that it is important to make sure you get enough of.

Fats

Fats fall into two categories: saturated and unsaturated fats. It is very important that a healthy balance is achieved within the diet. Fats are an essential part of the diet and a source of energy and provide essential fatty acids and fat–soluble vitamins. The right balance of fats should boost the body's immunity to infection and keep muscles, nerves and arteries in good condition. Most saturated fats are of animal origin and are hard when stored at room temperature. However, they can be found in plant-derived products such as palm oil, margarines and coconut oil, as well as in manufactured products such as pies, biscuits and cakes. A high intake of saturated fat over many years has been proven to increase heart disease and high blood cholesterol levels and often leads to weight gain. The aim of a healthy diet is to keep the fat content low in the foods that we eat. Lowering the amount of saturated fat that we consume is very important, but this this does not mean that it is good to consume lots of other types of fat.

There are two kinds of unsaturated fats: polyunsaturated fats and monounsaturated fats. Polyunsaturated fats include the following oils: safflower oil, soybean oil, corn oil and sesame oil. Within the polyunsaturated group are Omega oils. Omega-3 and omega-6 fats are essential for healthy cell function, energy and overall wellbeing. The omega-3 oils are of significant interest because they have been found to be particularly beneficial to coronary health and can encourage brain growth and development. While our modern diets contain plenty of omega-6, omega-3 can be harder to come by on a vegan diet, as it is typically derived from oily fish. For great health, focus on eating plenty of foods rich in omega-3, including ground flaxseed and chia seeds, spirulina, walnuts and hemp. Vegan omega-3 supplements can also be found at many health shops.

The most popular oils that are high in monounsaturates are olive oil, sunflower oil and peanut oil. The Mediterranean diet, which is based on foods high in monounsaturated fats, is recommended for heart health. Also, monounsaturated fats are known to help reduce the levels of LDL (the bad) cholesterol.

Proteins

Composed of amino acids (proteins' building bricks), proteins perform a wide variety of functions for the body, including supplying energy and building and repairing tissue. Vegan protein sources are abundant, although it is easy not to eat them if you don't know what they are. Plant-based sources of protein that you can enjoy in abundance include nuts and seeds, dark green leafy vegetables, quinoa, buckwheat, seitan, tempeh, soy protein (tofu, TVP) and rice combined with beans.

Nutrition

Minerals

∽ Calcium – Getting enough calcium on a vegan diet is actually surprisingly easy. Sources include kale, rocket, broccoli, butternut squash, parsley, oranges, nuts and seeds. Historically, spinach was thought to be a good source of calcium, but we now know that this isn't true – it contains oxalate, which in fact hinders the absorption of its calcium.

∽ Chromium – Part of the glucose tolerance factor, chromium balances blood sugar levels, helps to normalise hunger and reduce cravings, improves lifespan, helps protect DNA and is essential for heart function. Good sources are brewer's yeast, wholemeal bread, rye bread, potatoes, green peppers, and parsnips.

∽ Iodine – Important for thyroid hormones and for normal development. Seaweed is the best vegan source of iodine, but it can also be found in cranberries, potatoes, prunes, and other fruits and vegetables.

∽ Iron – As a component of haemoglobin, iron carries oxygen around the body. It is vital for normal growth and development. Getting enough iron means eating plenty of wholefoods. Plant-based sources of iron include dried fruits, dark green leafy vegetables, seeds, pulses, potatoes and whole grains. Vitamin C is needed to maximize iron absorption, so combine these ingredients with vitamin C-rich foods, such as oranges, blackcurrants, broccoli, mango and parsley.

∽ Magnesium – Important for efficient functioning of metabolic enzymes and development of the skeleton. Magnesium promotes healthy muscles by helping them to relax and is therefore good for PMS. It is also important for heart muscles and the nervous system. Good vegan sources are nuts, green vegetables and cereals.

~ **Phosphorus** – Forms and maintains bones and teeth, builds muscle tissue, helps maintain the body's pH and aids metabolism and energy production. Phosphorus is present in almost all foods.

~ **Potassium** – Enables nutrients to move into cells, while waste products move out; promotes healthy nerves and muscles; maintains fluid balance in the body; helps secretion of insulin for blood sugar control to produce constant energy; relaxes muscles; maintains heart functioning and stimulates gut movement to encourage proper elimination. Good vegan sources are fruit, vegetables and bread.

~ **Selenium** – Antioxidant properties help to protect against free radicals and carcinogens. Selenium reduces inflammation, stimulates the immune system to fight infections, promotes a healthy heart and helps vitamin E's action. It is also required for the male reproductive system and is needed for metabolism. Good sources are eggs, cereals, nuts and dairy products.

~ **Sodium** – Helps to control body fluid and balance, preventing dehydration. Sodium is involved in muscle and nerve function and helps move nutrients into cells. All foods are good sources, but pickled and salted foods are richest in sodium.

~ **Zinc** – Important for metabolism and the healing of wounds. It also aids ability to cope with stress, promotes a healthy nervous system and brain, especially in the growing foetus, aids bone and tooth formation and is essential for constant energy. Good sources are pulses, wholegrain cereals and nuts.

Vitamins

~ **Vitamin A** – Important for cell growth and development and for the formation of visual pigments in the eye. Found in red and yellow fruits and carrots.

- **Vitamin B1** – Important in releasing energy from carbohydrate-containing foods. Good sources are yeast and yeast products, bread, fortified breakfast cereals and potatoes.

- **Vitamin B2** – Important for metabolism of proteins, fats and carbohydrates. Found in yeast extract and fortified cereals.

- **Vitamin B3** – Helps the metabolism of food into energy. Vegan sources include fortified breakfast cereals and pulses.

- **Vitamin B5** – Important for the metabolism of food and energy production. All foods are good sources, but especially fortified breakfast cereals and wholegrain bread.

- **Vitamin B6** – Important for metabolism of protein and fat. Vitamin B6 may also be involved with the regulation of sex hormones. Good sources are soya beans and peanuts.

- **Vitamin B12** – As a vegan, you cannot get adequate amounts of B12 through your diet. It is essential to supplement with B12 patches, a sublingual spray and/or consistent consumption of foods fortified with B12. Have your B12 levels tested regularly to make sure you are not deficient in this essential vitamin.

- **Biotin** – Important for metabolism of fatty acids. Nuts are a good vegan source of biotin. Micro-organisms also manufacture this vitamin in the gut.

- **Vitamin C** – Important for healing wounds and the formation of collagen, which keeps skin and bones strong. It is an important antioxidant. Sources are fruits and vegetables.

- **Vitamin D** – Vitamin D teams up with calcium for strong, healthy bones. While much of our vitamin D comes through skin exposure to the sun, most people do not get enough sunlight for adequate vitamin D absorption. As the main dietary source for this important vitamin is fatty fish, vegans are particularly susceptible to deficiency, so may need to take supplements. Make sure they are vegan, as many are not.

- ∾ Vitamin E – Important as an antioxidant vitamin, helping to protect cell membranes from damage. Good vegan sources are vegetable oils, margarines, seeds, nuts and green vegetables.

- ∾ Folic Acid – Critical during pregnancy for the development of foetus brain and nerves. It is essential for brain and nerve function and is needed for protein and red blood cell formation. Sources are wholegrain cereals, fortified cereals, green, leafy vegetables and oranges.

- ∾ Vitamin K – Important for controlling blood clotting. Sources are cauliflower, Brussels sprouts, lettuce, cabbage, beans, broccoli, peas, asparagus, potatoes, corn oil, and tomatoes.

Carbohydrates

Carbohydrates come in two basic forms: starchy and sugar carbohydrates. Starchy carbohydrates, also known as complex carbohydrates, include cereals, potatoes, breads, rice and pasta. Eating wholegrain varieties also provides fibre, beneficial in preventing bowel cancer, and controlling cholesterol. Sugar carbohydrates, known as fast-release carbohydrates (because of the quick fix of energy they give), include sugar and sugar-sweetened products such as jams and syrups. Fruits provide fructose, which is fruit sugar.

∾ Nutrition

Key Vegan Foods

F resh produce should be the staple element of a healthy vegan diet, but you should also stock up on storecupboard ingredients in order to get the most out of what veganism has to offer. Vegan alternatives and pre-packaged foods also have a part to play.

Fresh Ingredients

Fruits and vegetables will give you energy as well as helping you maintain a healthy weight. This is where many of your essential nutrients come from. Eat a rainbow of colours for a broad spectrum of vitamins and minerals.

∽ Herbs & Spices – Fresh herbs and spices introduce the potential for exotic and international flavours to be created simply and quickly. Have you tried fresh Thai curry paste, made with fresh ginger, garlic, chilli, coriander and lime? Or an Italian bake with fresh oregano?

∽ Vegetables – Vegetables come in all shapes and sizes. They can be eaten raw, lightly cooked, stewed or baked – there is so much creativity at your fingertips! Whether you grow your own, buy from farmers' markets or the superstore, make veggies a major part of your vegan diet. From roots and tubers, to leaves, to veggie fruits; from brassicas to alliums to fungi; the variety available to us today is breathtaking. Their amazing flavours, textures and colours provide us with life-giving nutrients.

∽ Fruit – Fruit is a major source of healthy carbohydrate. It is hydrating, full of vitamins and incredibly diverse in its uses. On a vegan diet, you can enjoy it as a light breakfast, added to cooked porridge, served in savoury salads, and in a wide range of desserts. It is important to eat a range of fruit – each colour represents a different nutritional component, and we need a wide spectrum of vitamins and minerals for optimum mental and physical health. If you want to, stick to low glycaemic fruits, such as fresh berries, citrus and orchard fruit like apples and nectarines.

Storecupboard Ingredients

As a vegan cook, you will be happiest when your cupboards are stocked with dried goods and bottled ingredients, allowing you to create something delicious, even when you are out of fresh produce. You will use these ingredients in everything, from savoury and sweet breakfasts, to light lunches and hearty evening meals.

∽ Nuts & Seeds – Nuts and seeds are a great source of protein. They are also a fantastic source of essential healthy fats. You can make delicious vegan milks and cheese substitutes with them, as well as adding nuts and seeds to your breakfasts, smoothies, and sweet and savoury recipes for added texture and flavour.

∽ Beans, Pulses & Legumes – Beans, pulses and legumes are a staple part of most vegan diets. They bring a satisfying texture and flavour to any dish, and can be whizzed up into dips and soups to make a filling light meal. Beans, pulses and legumes include lentils, chickpeas, kidney beans, butter beans, soya beans, haricot beans, black beans, cannellini beans, split peas and mung beans. Most beans and pulses need to be pre-soaked before cooking. Lentils are an exception to this rule and can be cooked without soaking. They are often a favourite for their flavour and speed of cooking, compared with other dried beans.

❧ Herbs, Spices & Condiments – Investing in staple dried herbs and spices will open up a wide range of vegan recipes. Popular herbs in vegan cooking include oregano, thyme, bay leaves, sage, parsley and Italian mixed herbs. Spices for vegan dishes include curry powders, ground cumin, ground coriander, smoked paprika, turmeric, mustard seeds, pepper, good-quality mineral salt, cinnamon, nutmeg, vanilla extract and cardamom. With vegan condiments you can bring depth and added flavour to your recipes. Favourites include soy sauce and tamari, mustard, nutritional yeast flakes, sun-dried tomato paste, vegetable bouillon, hot chili sauce, barbecue sauce, ketchup, vegan mayonnaise and vegan Worcestershire sauce.

❧ Oils – Most plant-derived oils are highly processed and toxic to the body when cooked. Healthy oils include extra-virgin coconut and olive oils. Other cold-pressed oils that are super good for vegans when used raw, delicious in salad dressings and drizzled straight over cooked food, include hemp oil, flaxseed oil and avocado oil.

❧ Vinegars – Vinegar is vegan and there is a wide range of delicious options available. Use vinegar in salad dressings, in marinades for vegetables, tofu and tempeh, and to flavour dishes. Favourite types of vinegar include balsamic vinegar, red or white wine vinegar and apple cider vinegar.

❧ Vegan Sweeteners – Apart from honey, most sweeteners are vegan, but many are not good for you and their mass production causes harm to our planet. There are many healthy, plant-based sweeteners that have a lesser impact on the environment and can be easily used in baking, in desserts and as a condiment. Avoid artificial sweeteners completely. More and more research is coming to light about the damaging effects of artificial sweeteners on our long-term health. Favourite healthy vegan sweeteners include coconut sugar, maple syrup, date syrup and stevia. Try to use them when possible if you want to be a healthy vegan.

- ✺ Grains – Grains are another staple in the vegan diet. Although they contain many essential nutrients, it is easy to overeat grains, particularly wheat. Many people are intolerant to wheat without realizing, so keep it to a minimum and, if you can, find products using older strains of wheat – such as spelt, which has been found to be more easily digested by many people. Your body will thank you for it!

Other delicious grains that work beautifully on a vegan diet include oats, rice, quinoa, millet, amaranth, barley and corn. Cook them in their whole form to use in savoury dishes, or use the rolled versions in breakfast porridge, muesli and granola.

Vegan Alternatives

- ✺ Dairy Substitutes – There are vegan substitutes for milk, butter, cheese and yogurt available in most superstores and health food stores. Milk substitutes usually come as tetra-packed, plant-based milks such as rice milk, oat milk, soya milk, almond milk and coconut milk. Try them out to see which one works for you. Vegan margarine-like spreads are made from emulsified plant oils and other ingredients. With pre-packaged cheese substitutes, be aware that some brands are better than others for that melted-cheese effect. Vegan yogurt is usually made from soy or coconut milk. *See* pages 34, 36 and 40 for how to make your own delicious dairy alternatives.

- ✺ Egg Substitutes – You can buy vegan 'egg-replacer' for use in baking and desserts, or you can make your own. To replace one egg:

1 tablespoon ground flaxseed
3 tablespoons water

Combine the ground flaxseed and water, and use when required. Adjust the recipe proportionately according to the number of eggs needed.

Key Vegan Foods

~ Meat Substitutes – These days, there are vegan substitutes for most flavours of meat, from bacon to sausages, burgers to chicken. More generic meat substitutes include TVP (textured vegetable protein), made from soy; tempeh, made from fermented whole soya beans; and seitan, which is made from wheat flour – all of which you can flavour yourself. Another meat substitute you may be aware of is the 'mycoprotein'-based Quorn – unfortunately, many of Quorn's products are not vegan as they contain egg, though they do now have a vegan range.

Pre-packaged Foods

There is a huge selection of pre-packaged vegan foods available. Veganism has become more mainstream and the food industry has stepped up to provide for this niche. Pre-packaged vegan foods range from the dairy, meat and milk substitutes already mentioned to ingredients such as tofu, vegan mayonnaise, dips, ready-prepared meals, vegan ice cream, desserts, chocolate and sweets. This is part of the reason it is easy to be a 'junk' vegan. Although it costs more, the convenience is undeniable. As long as the focus is on a balanced, mainly wholefood vegan diet, enjoy your favourite pre-packaged foods guilt-free.

Foods to Avoid

It is not always obvious which foods contain animal products. Here are some ingredients that may catch you out:

~ Gelatine – Made from the connective tissue of pigs and cows – used in many sweets, as well as in jelly.

- **Refined sugar** – This can be lightened with bone char, derived from the bones of cattle.

- **Additives** – Certain food additives, including E120, E322, E422, E471, E542, E631, E901 and E904, are sometimes derived from animals.

- **Cochineal** – Also known as carmine, this red food colouring is made from insects.

- **Isinglass** – Made from fish bladders, this is often used in beer and wine-making.

- **Omega-3 and Vitamin D3** – Products enriched with omega-3 and vitamin D3 usually use animal sources for these nutrients.

- **Shellac** – This insect-based product, is sometimes used to wax fresh produce such as fruit or to glaze sweets.

- **Whey, casein and lactose** – these common additives in many pre-packaged foods, are all derived from dairy.

- **L-cysteine** – Some bread products contain L-cysteine, which often comes from feathers, to keep them soft.

- **Anchovies** – Olive tapenade often contains anchovies, as do some condiments and ready-made sauces.

- **Batter** –The batter on deep-fried foods often contains eggs.

- **Pasta** – Pasta, especially fresh pasta, often contains eggs.

As a rule, look for brands or products that are marked 'cruelty-free' or 'vegan' and read the ingredients labels on other foods to make sure that they don't contain animal products.

Key Vegan Foods

Basics & Breakfast

Being Vegan doesn't have to mean missing out on the delights of traditional dairy- and egg-filled breakfast items – check out our nutritious Quinoa Porridge with Berries or the indulgent French Toast, or for a more savoury brunch try the inspired Breakfast Tacos. This chapter also features some key basic recipes for home-made staples such as dairy-free milks and yogurt, which will save you a fortune on shop-bought products.

Almond, Oat & Rice Milks

Makes 750 ml/1¹/₄ pints

For the oat milk

75 g/3 oz rolled oats
750 ml/1¼ pints water

For the rice milk

150 g/5 oz cooked brown rice
750 ml/1¼ pints water

For the raw almond milk

225 g/8 oz whole almonds, soaked
overnight and rinsed
750 ml/1¼ pints water

For the optional flavouring

1–2 tsp maple syrup
½ tsp vanilla extract

Blend your chosen milk ingredients in a blender until smooth and creamy.

For the first strain, pour the mixture into a sieve, and use a spoon to scrape the bottom of the sieve to keep the milk straining through.

If you like your milk silky smooth, strain again using a nut milk bag, fine cloth or clean tea towel. Line a large bowl or jug with the cloth and pour the mixture into the cloth. Pull up the edges of the cloth and hold them in your hand, so that the mixture strains into the bowl. Use your other hand to squeeze the mixture through the cloth. Milk will last 1–2 days in the refrigerator, so make it fresh or freeze in small batches.

Plant-based Buttery Spread

Makes 200 ml/7 fl oz

125 g/4 oz coconut oil
50 ml/2 fl oz light olive oil
pinch salt
2 tbsp macadamia nuts or pine nuts

Melt the coconut oil in a pan over a low heat. Once melted, add to a blender with the remaining ingredients and blend until smooth.

Transfer to a sterilized jar and store in the refrigerator for up to a month. Many of the vegan butter alternatives aren't that good for you, but this one is, and it tastes divine too.

Vegan Mayonnaise

Makes about 250 ml/8 fl oz

225 g/8 oz silken tofu, drained
2 tbsp light olive oil
1 tbsp lemon juice
½ tsp salt
1 tsp Dijon mustard

Blend all the ingredients in a blender until smooth and creamy. Store in the refrigerator for up to a week. For added excitement add garlic, fresh herbs or spices.

Vegan Yogurt

Serves 2

400 ml/14 fl oz can coconut milk
4 capsules acidophilus probiotic
(available from any good health
food store)
½ tsp xanthan gum

Preheat a thermos flask.

Heat the milk in a very clean pan until just warm (do not overheat – you want it to be just warm to the touch), then pour into a blender with the acidophilus and xanthan gum and blend until smooth.

Pour the mixture into the preheated flask and leave for 12 hours. After 12 hours, the yogurt is ready. Pour into sterilized jars. Chill for up to 10 days.

Note: To make a large batch, adjust the recipe proportionately and pour the mixture into sterilized glass jars in the oven, with just the light on, for 12 hours. The heat from the light is enough to culture the yogurt.

Vegan Custard

**Serves 1 as a dessert
or 3 as a sauce**

300 ml/10 fl oz unsweetened almond, rice
or oat milk (*see* page 34)
1 tbsp cornflour
1 tsp vanilla extract
50 g/2 oz sugar
pinch salt
pinch ground turmeric (optional)

Set 3 tablespoons milk aside. Heat the remaining milk in a pan until just before boiling.

Place the remaining ingredients with 1 tablespoon of the reserved milk in a heatproof bowl and mix thoroughly. Add another tablespoon of milk and mix thoroughly, making sure there are no lumps, before adding the final tablespoon.

Slowly pour the hot milk over the ingredients, stirring, then return the mixture to the pan and bring to the boil, stirring constantly to stop it sticking. Serve.

Cheeze Sauce

Makes 300 ml/¹/₂ pint

250 ml/8 fl oz water
130 g/4½ oz cashew nuts
1 tbsp lemon juice
2 spring onions chopped
2 tbsp nutritional yeast flakes
¾ tsp salt

Blend all the ingredients together until smooth, then gently heat in a pan until thick and creamy. This simple dairy-free cheeze sauce can be poured over steamed vegetables and rice, or stirred through pasta or served as a hot dip with Rainbow Oven Fries (*see* page 62)

Dairy-free Tzatziki

**Serves 4 as a dip
or side dish**

1 cucumber, peeled and coarsely grated
1 tsp salt
300 g/11 oz vegan yogurt (*see* page 40)
2 garlic cloves, peeled and crushed
2 tbsp olive oil
2 tsp lemon juice
1 tsp chopped mint
1 tsp chopped dill
freshly ground black pepper
crusty bread or crudités, to serve

Place the cucumber in a sieve set over a bowl and sprinkle with ½ teaspoon of the salt. Leave to stand.

Mix the remaining salt with the yogurt, garlic, oil, lemon juice and chopped herbs.

Using your hand or the back of a spoon, squeeze the grated cucumber against the sides of the sieve to remove as much cucumber juice as possible. Stir the squeezed cucumber through the yogurt mix. Season with pepper and chill for a few hours. Serve as a dip with crusty bread or crudités. Chill for up to 48 hours.

Overnight Breakfast Pot

Serves 1

50 g/2 oz rolled oats
1 tbsp chia seeds
1 handful goji berries
300 ml/10 fl oz unsweetened almond milk
fresh fruit of choice, such as apricots
or nectarines

Mix the oats, chia seeds, goji berries and milk together and pour into a glass jar or bowl. Chill overnight.

The next morning, stir the oat mixture and top with fruit. This beautiful breakfast is jam-packed with superfood goodness and is sure to get your day off to a brilliant start.

Berry Power Smoothie Bowl

Serves 1

For the smoothie

65 ml/2½ fl oz water
4 handfuls frozen mixed berries
1 ripe banana, peeled
½ tsp açaí powder (optional)

To serve

1 small handful sliced toasted almonds
1 small handful fresh berries, such as
blackberries and blueberries
1 banana, peeled and sliced
1 tbsp pumpkin seeds
½ tbsp chia seeds

This bowl is packed full of all the goodness of a smoothie, with the added bonus of being more substantial, to fill you up. Put all the smoothie ingredients in a blender and blend until smooth. Pour into a bowl and serve, topped with almonds, fruit and seeds.

Quinoa Porridge with Berries

Serves 1

250 ml/8 fl oz unsweetened dairy-free milk
pinch salt (optional)
½ tsp vanilla extract
1 tbsp unrefined granulated sugar
or maple syrup
40 g/1½ oz quinoa flakes
1 handful frozen berries
1 handful fresh blueberries
mint leaves (optional)

Combine the milk, salt (if using), vanilla and sugar in a pan. Bring to the boil, stirring. Once the milk is boiling, stir in the quinoa. Turn off the heat and leave for 3 minutes until soft and creamy. Pour into a bowl and top with berries and mint, if liked.

Breakfast Pancakes

Makes 8 pancakes

For the pancakes

200 g/7 oz plain flour
1 tbsp ground flaxseed
2 tsp baking powder
¼ tsp salt
1 tsp unrefined granulated sugar
or maple syrup
300 ml/10 fl oz unsweetened dairy-free milk
1 tsp vanilla extract
coconut oil, for cooking

For the topping

4 tbsp strawberry or raspberry jam
1 handful desiccated coconut
2 tbsp water
2 handfuls blueberries
2 handfuls strawberries, halved

For the topping, heat the jam, coconut and water in a small pan, stirring to combine, then set aside. Preheat the oven to its lowest temperature. Blend all the pancake ingredients, except the oil, until smooth. Heat a little oil in a frying pan over a medium-high heat.

Ladle 4 tablespoons of batter at a time into the pan, allowing each pancake to spread naturally. Cook for 3 minutes on each side until lightly browned. Once cooked, keep warm in the oven while you cook the next batch. Top with the sauce and fruit.

French Toast

Serves 2

125 ml/4 fl oz unsweetened dairy-free milk
3 tbsp plain flour
1 tbsp maple syrup, plus extra for drizzling
½ tsp ground cinnamon
½ tsp vanilla extract
4 thick slices bread
coconut oil, for frying
1 handful blueberries
icing sugar (optional)

Whisk the milk, flour, maple syrup, cinnamon and vanilla together, then pour the mixture into a wide shallow dish. Quickly dip both sides of the bread into the batter – don't let the slices get too soggy.

Heat 2 tablespoons oil in a frying pan over a medium-high heat and cook the French toast for 3 minutes on each side until golden brown. Add more oil, if necessary. Serve drizzled with maple syrup and topped with blueberries. Dust with icing sugar, if liked.

Breakfast Tacos

Serves 1

2 small flour tortillas
200 g/7 oz canned spicy mixed beans
(check the label to make sure they
are vegan)
½ ripe avocado, sliced
50 g/2 oz grated vegan cheese

For the salsa verde

½ garlic clove, peeled and
very finely chopped
2 tsp capers
2 tbsp finely chopped parsley
2 tbsp finely chopped basil
2 tbsp finely chopped mint
½ tsp Dijon mustard
2 tsp white wine vinegar
1 tbsp olive oil
freshly ground black pepper

Mix all the salsa ingredients together in a bowl and leave to stand. Lightly heat the tortillas in a frying pan. Serve topped with the mixed beans, avocado, grated cheese and salsa verde.

Tip: If you are doing a taco brunch, wrap all the tortillas in foil and put them in the oven preheated to 150°C/300°F/Gas Mark 2 for 20 minutes before serving.

Snacks & Sides

If you're on the hunt for snacks that satisfy or sides and starters to compliment any meal, look no further. If you're in the mood for sophisticated starters, try the Hot Grilled Chicory & Pears; if you crave colour and freshness, check out the Rainbow Summer Rolls; if you need a handy lunch for the office, give the Seitan Burrito Wraps a go; or if it's movie night, why not indulge in some Nacho 'Cheese' Popcorn?

Rainbow Oven Fries

Makes 1 big plate of fries

2 potatoes, peeled
1 large beetroot, peeled
1 sweet potato, peeled
1 carrot, peeled
1 large parsnip, peeled
3 tbsp olive oil
½ tsp medium hot chili powder (optional)
salt
Cheeze Sauce (*see* page 44)
or tomato ketchup, to serve

Preheat the oven to 200°C/400°F/Gas Mark 6. Cut each vegetable lengthways into 1 cm/½ inch thick slices, then cut each slice into 1 cm/½ inch fries. Toss the fries with the remaining ingredients, then arrange in a single layer in 1–2 baking dishes. Bake for 45 minutes, turning them over every 15 minutes until lightly browned and cooked. Serve with Cheeze Sauce or ketchup.

Potato Dauphinoise

Serves 8

3 garlic cloves, peeled
500 ml/18 fl oz soy cream
500 ml/18 fl oz unsweetened almond
or soya milk
large pinch salt
8 large King Edward or Maris Piper
potatoes, peeled and very thinly sliced,
about 3 mm/⅛ inch thick

Preheat the oven to 190°C/375°F/Gas Mark 5.

Gently squash the garlic with the back of a wooden spoon. Put the cream, milk, garlic and salt into a large pan and bring to a simmer. Add the potatoes and simmer, gently stirring, for 3 minutes until just cooked.

Remove the potatoes with a slotted spoon and place them in a shallow ovenproof dish so that they are about 5 cm/2 inches in depth. Discard the garlic from the sauce and pour over the potatoes, just enough to cover all the slices. Bake for 30 minutes until the potatoes are soft and browned on top.

Tip: Freeze any extra sauce for adding to soup or pasta dishes.

Vegetable Samosas

Serves 4–6

150 g/5 oz potatoes, peeled
2–3 tbsp vegetable oil, plus extra
for deep-frying
1 tsp mustard seeds
1 onion, peeled and chopped
1 tsp ground coriander
½–1 tsp garam masala
½ tsp turmeric
1–2 red chillies, deseeded and chopped
2 tbsp water
1 large carrot, peeled and grated
75 g/3 oz frozen peas
75 g/3 oz French beans, trimmed
and chopped
250 g/9 oz filo pastry

Cut the potato into small dice and leave in a bowl of cold water until required. Drain thoroughly and shake dry when ready to use.

Heat 2 tablespoons of the oil in a frying pan, add the mustard seeds and stir-fry for 1 minute, or until they pop. Add the onion and continue to fry for 5–8 minutes, or until softened. Add the remaining oil, if necessary.

Add the spices, chilli and water and cook for a further 3 minutes, then add the potatoes, carrot, peas and beans. Stir, then cover and cook for 10–15 minutes, or until the vegetables are just cooked. Allow to cool.

Cut the pastry into 7.5 cm/3 inch strips. Brush a strip lightly with water and place a second strip on top. Place 1 tablespoon of the filling at one end of the strip then fold the pastry over to form a triangle. Brush the pastry lightly with water. Continue folding the pastry forming triangles to the end of the strip. Repeat with the remaining pastry and filling.

Heat the oil in a deep-fryer to a temperature of 180°C/350°F and deep-fry the samosas, in batches of about 2 or 3 at a time, for 2–3 minutes, or until golden. Remove with a slotted spoon and drain on absorbent kitchen paper. Serve hot or cold. **Note:** This recipe also works well with other ingredients – try chickpeas with spinach, onion, chopped red pepper and carrot.

Nacho Cheese Popcorn

Makes 1 large bowl

2 tbsp coconut oil
40 g/1½ oz popping corn

For the seasoning

2 tbsp coconut oil
1 garlic clove, peeled and crushed
2 tbsp nutritional yeast flakes
1 tsp lime juice
¼ tsp smoked paprika
½ tsp unrefined salt

Use a large pan and get the oil really hot. Add 3 popping corn kernels. Once they have popped, the oil is hot enough. Add the remaining corn. Cover, reduce the heat to low and cook until the corn stops popping, shaking the pan regularly. Once the popping stops, uncover.

Mix all the seasoning ingredients together. Add the popcorn and mix to co

Wok-Fried Garlic Chili Popcorn & Sesame-Coated Pecans

Serves 4–6

For the popcorn

75 ml/3 fl oz vegetable oil
75 g/3 oz unpopped popcorn
½ tsp garlic salt
1 tsp hot chilli powder

For the pecans

50 g/2 oz sugar
½ tsp ground cinnamon
½ tsp ground Chinese five spice powder
¼ tsp salt
¼ tsp cayenne pepper
175 g/6 oz pecan or walnut halves
sesame seeds for sprinkling

For the popcorn, heat half the oil in a large wok over a medium-high heat. Add 2–3 kernels and cover with a lid. When these kernels pop, add all the popcorn and cover tightly. Cook until the popping stops, shaking from time to time.

When the popping stops, pour the popped corn into a bowl and immediately add the remaining oil to the wok with the garlic salt and chilli powder. Stir-fry for 30 seconds, or until blended and fragrant.

Return the popcorn to the wok, stir-fry and toss for a further 30 seconds, or until coated. Pour into the bowl and serve warm or at room temperature.

For the pecans, put the sugar, cinnamon, Chinese five spice powder, salt and cayenne pepper into a large wok and stir in 50 ml/2 fl oz water. Bring to the boil over a high heat, then simmer for 4 minutes, stirring frequently.

Remove from the heat and stir in the pecans or walnuts until well coated. Turn onto a lightly oiled, non-stick baking sheet and sprinkle generously with the sesame seeds.

Working quickly with 2 forks, separate the nuts into individual pieces or bite-sized clusters. Sprinkle with a few more sesame seeds and leave to cool completely. Carefully remove from the baking sheet, breaking into smaller pieces if necessary.

Hot Grilled Chicory & Pears

Serves 4

50 g/2 oz unblanched almonds,
roughly chopped
4 small heads of chicory
2 tbsp olive oil
1 tbsp walnut oil
2 firm ripe dessert pears
2 tsp lemon juice
1 tsp freshly chopped oregano.
salt and freshly ground black pepper
freshly chopped oregano, to garnish
warmed ciabatta bread, to serve

Preheat grill. Spread the chopped almonds in a single layer on the grill pan. Cook under a hot grill for about 3 minutes, moving the almonds around occasionally, until lightly browned. Reserve.

Halve the chicory lengthways and cut out the cores. Mix together the olive and walnut oils. Brush about 2 tablespoons all over the chicory.

Put the chicory in a grill pan, cut-side up and cook under a hot grill for 2–3 minutes, or until beginning to char. Turn and cook for a further 1–2 minutes, then turn again.

Peel, core and thickly slice the pears. Brush with 1 tablespoon of the oils, then place the pears on top of the chicory. Grill for a further 3–4 minutes, or until both the chicory and pears are soft.

Transfer the chicory and pears to 4 warmed serving plates. Whisk together the remaining oil, lemon juice and oregano and season to taste with salt and pepper.

Drizzle the dressing over the chicory and pears and scatter with the toasted almonds. Garnish with fresh oregano and serve with ciabatta bread.

Vegetable Tempura

Serves 4–6

125 g/4 oz rice flour
75 g/3 oz plain flour
4 tsp baking powder
1 tbsp dried mustard powder
2 tsp semolina
salt and freshly ground black pepper
300 ml/½ pint groundnut oil
125 g/4 oz courgette, trimmed
and thickly sliced
125 g/4 oz mangetout
125 g/4 oz baby sweetcorn
4 small red onions, peeled and quartered
1 large red pepper, deseeded and cut into
2.5 cm/1 inch wide strips
light soy sauce, to serve

Sift the rice flour and the plain flour into a large bowl, then sift in the baking powder and dried mustard powder.

Stir the semolina into the flour mixture and season to taste with salt and pepper. Gradually beat in 300 ml/½ pint cold water to produce a thin coating batter. Leave to stand at room temperature for 30 minutes.

Heat a wok or large frying pan, add the oil and heat to 180°C/350°F. Working in batches and using a slotted spoon, dip the vegetables in the batter until well coated, then drop them carefully into the hot oil. Cook each batch for 2–3 minutes or until golden. Drain on absorbent kitchen paper and keep warm while cooking the remaining batches.

Transfer the vegetables to a warmed serving platter and serve immediately with the light soy sauce to use as a dipping sauce.

Paprika Tomatoes on Toast

Serves 2

1 tbsp olive oil
1 spring onion, chopped
2 tomatoes, chopped
1 tbsp dried oregano
¼ tsp smoked paprika
pinch unrefined granulated sugar
¼ tsp unrefined salt
4 sun-dried tomato halves, in oil or rehydrated, chopped
1 thick slice white or brown bread, chopped
3 tbsp toasted almonds
freshly ground black pepper
4 slices toast
flat-leaf parsley, to garnish (optional)

Heat the oil in a frying pan over a medium-low heat and fry the spring onions for 5 minutes until soft. Add the chopped tomatoes, oregano, paprika, sugar and salt, increase the heat to medium and simmer for 5 minutes. Transfer to a food processor, add the sun-dried tomatoes, bread, almonds and pepper and blitz until well combined but still with texture.

Serve on toast, topped with parsley, if liked. For a lighter alternative, try this richly satisfying spread on rice cakes or oatcakes.

Italian Baked Tomatoes with Curly Endive & Radicchio

Serves 4

1 tsp olive oil
4 beef tomatoes
salt
50 g/2 oz fresh white breadcrumbs
1 tbsp freshly snipped chives
1 tbsp freshly chopped parsley
125 g/4 oz button mushrooms, finely chopped
salt and freshly ground black pepper
25 g/1 oz fresh Parmesan-style
vegan cheese, grated

For the salad

½ curly endive lettuce
½ small piece of radicchio
2 tbsp olive oil
1 tsp balsamic vinegar
salt and freshly ground black pepper

Preheat oven to 190°C/375°F/Gas Mark 5. Lightly oil a baking tray with the teaspoon of oil. Slice the tops off the tomatoes and remove all the tomato flesh and sieve into a large bowl. Sprinkle a little salt inside the tomato shells and then place them upside down on a plate while the filling is prepared.

Mix the sieved tomato with the breadcrumbs, fresh herbs and mushrooms and season well with salt and pepper. Place the tomato shells on the prepared baking tray and fill with the tomato and mushroom mixture.

Sprinkle the vegan cheese on the top and bake in the preheated oven for 15–20 minutes, until golden brown.

Meanwhile, prepare the salad. Arrange the endive and radicchio on individual serving plates and mix the remaining ingredients together in a small bowl to make the dressing. Season to taste.

When the tomatoes are cooked, allow to rest for 5 minutes, then place on the prepared plates and drizzle over a little dressing. Serve warm.

Mushroom & Red Wine Pâté

Serves 4

3 large slices of white bread, crusts removed
2 tsp oil
1 small onion, peeled and finely chopped
1 garlic clove, peeled and crushed
350 g/12 oz button mushrooms,
wiped and finely chopped
150 ml/¼ pint vegan red wine
½ tsp dried mixed herbs
1 tbsp freshly chopped parsley
salt and freshly ground black pepper
2 tbsp low-fat vegan cream cheese

To serve

finely chopped cucumber
finely chopped tomato

Preheat the oven to 180°C/350°F/Gas Mark 4. Cut the bread in half diagonally. Place the bread triangles on a baking tray and cook for 10 minutes.

Remove from the oven and split each bread triangle in half to make 12 triangles and return to the oven until golden and crisp. Leave to cool on a wire rack.

Heat the oil in a saucepan and gently cook the onion and garlic until transparent.

Add the mushrooms and cook, stirring for 3–4 minutes or until the mushroom juices start to run.

Stir the wine and herbs into the mushroom mixture and bring to the boil. Reduce the heat and simmer uncovered until all the liquid is absorbed.

Remove from the heat and season to taste with salt and pepper. Leave to cool.

When cold, beat in the vegan cream cheese and adjust the seasoning. Place in a small clean bowl and chill until required. Serve the toast triangles with the cucumber and tomato.

Seitan Burrito Wraps

Serves 1

For the guacamole
½ ripe avocado
½ lime
1 large pinch salt

For the Pico de Gallo
1 tomato, diced
2.5 cm/1 inch piece cucumber, diced
¼ small red onion, diced
1 tbsp chopped coriander

For the wrap
1 tbsp olive oil
2 seitan slices (available in most
good health food shops)
1 large flour tortilla wrap

For the guacamole, mash the avocado with the lime and salt. For the Pico de Gallo, combine all the ingredients together.

For the wrap, heat the oil in a frying pan over a medium heat and fry the seitan for 3 minutes on each side. Lay the tortilla on a flat surface. Distribute the guacamole, Pico de Gallo and seitan over the wrap, leaving the ends bare. Roll up, folding in the ends to stop the filling falling out. Cut diagonally across the centre before serving.

Vegetables Braised in Olive Oil & Lemon

Serves 4

small strip of pared rind and juice
of ½ lemon
4 tbsp olive oil
1 bay leaf
large sprig of thyme
150 ml/¼ pint water
4 spring onions, trimmed and finely chopped
175 g/6 oz baby button mushrooms
175 g/6 oz broccoli, cut into small florets
175 g/6 oz cauliflower, cut into small florets
1 medium courgette, sliced on the diagonal
2 tbsp freshly snipped chives
salt and freshly ground black pepper
lemon zest, to garnish

Put the pared lemon rind and juice into a large saucepan. Add the olive oil, bay leaf, thyme and the water. Bring to the boil. Add the spring onions and mushrooms. Top with the broccoli and cauliflower, trying to add them so that the stalks are submerged in the water and the tops are just above it. Cover and simmer for 3 minutes.

Scatter the courgettes on top, so that they are steamed rather than boiled. Cook, covered, for a further 3–4 minutes, until all the vegetables are tender. Using a slotted spoon, transfer the vegetables from the liquid into a warmed serving dish. Increase the heat and boil rapidly for 3–4 minutes, or until the liquid is reduced to about 8 tablespoons. Remove the lemon rind, bay leaf and thyme sprig and discard.

Stir the chives into the reduced liquid, season to taste with salt and pepper and pour over the vegetables. Sprinkle with lemon zest and serve immediately.

Vegetable Thai Spring Rolls

Serves 4

50 g/2 oz cellophane vermicelli
4 dried shiitake mushrooms
1 tbsp groundnut oil
2 medium carrots, peeled and cut into
fine matchsticks
125 g/4 oz mangetout, cut lengthways
into fine strips
3 spring onions, trimmed and chopped
125 g/4 oz canned bamboo shoots,
cut into fine matchsticks
1 cm/½ inch piece fresh root ginger,
peeled and grated
1 tbsp light soy sauce
1 portion egg-replacer, halved (*see* page 29)
salt and freshly ground black pepper
20 spring roll wrappers, each about
12.5 cm/5 inch square
vegetable oil for deep-frying
spring onion tassels, to garnish

Place the vermicelli in a bowl and pour over enough boiling water to cover. Leave to soak for 5 minutes or until softened, then drain. Cut into 7.5 cm/3 inch lengths. Soak the shiitake mushrooms in almost boiling water for 15 minutes, drain, discard the stalks and slice thinly.

Heat a wok or large frying pan, add the groundnut oil and when hot, add the carrots and stir-fry for 1 minute. Add the mangetout and spring onions and stir-fry for 2–3 minutes or until tender. Tip the vegetables into a bowl and leave to cool.

Stir the vermicelli and shiitake mushrooms into the cooled vegetables with the bamboo shoots, ginger, soy sauce and half of the egg-replacer. Season to taste with salt and pepper and mix thoroughly.

Brush the edges of a spring roll wrapper with a little beaten egg-replacer. Spoon 2 teaspoons of the vegetable filling on to the wrapper, in a 7.5 cm/3 inch log shape 2.5 cm/1 inch from one edge. Fold the wrapper edge over the filling, then fold in the right and left sides. Brush the folded edges with more egg-replacer and roll up neatly. Place on an oiled baking sheet, seam-side down and make the rest of the spring rolls.

Heat the oil in a heavy-based saucepan or deep-fat fryer to 180°C/350°F. Deep-fry the spring rolls, 6 at a time for 2–3 minutes, or until golden brown and crisp. Drain on absorbent kitchen paper and arrange on a warmed platter. Garnish with spring onion tassels and serve immediately.

Rainbow Summer Rolls

**Serves 2 as a main dish
or 4 as a starter**

4 large rice sheets
75 g/3 oz red cabbage, finely sliced
1 carrot, peeled and cut into julienne strips
1 red pepper, finely sliced
1 handful coriander
1 tbsp chia seeds (optional)

For the dipping sauce
4 tbsp soy sauce or tamari
1 tsp toasted sesame oil
2 tbsp rice vinegar
2 garlic cloves, peeled
1 mild red chili
4 pitted Medjool dates

For the dipping sauce, blend all the ingredients until smooth.

Rice sheets are available from Asian stores. Submerge each sheet in a bowl of hot water to soften it just before you are ready to use it.

Prepare one roll at a time as follows:

Carefully place a softened rice sheet on a flat surface.

Layer red cabbage, carrot, pepper, coriander and chia seeds along the centre of the sheet, leaving 2.5 cm/1 inch free at the ends. Don't overfill.

Roll into a tight sausage, encasing the filling and tucking the ends in to stop the filling from falling out.

Repeat with the remaining rice sheets.

Once all the rolls are completed, carefully cut each one in half diagonally and arrange on a plate. Serve with the dipping sauce.

Ginger & Garlic Potatoes

Serves 4

700 g/1½ lb potatoes
2.5 cm/1 inch piece of root ginger, peeled and coarsely chopped
3 garlic cloves, peeled and chopped
½ tsp turmeric
1 tsp salt
½ tsp cayenne pepper
5 tbsp vegetable oil
1 tsp whole fennel seeds
1 large eating apple, cored and diced
6 spring onions, trimmed and sliced diagonally
1 tbsp freshly chopped coriander

To serve

assorted bitter salad leaves
curry-flavoured mayonnaise

Scrub the potatoes, then place, unpeeled, in a large saucepan and cover with boiling salted water. Bring to the boil and cook for 15 minutes, then drain and leave the potatoes to cool completely. Peel and cut into 2.5 cm/1 inch cubes.

Place the root ginger, garlic, turmeric, salt and cayenne pepper in a food processor and blend for 1 minute. With the motor still running, slowly add 3 tablespoons of water and blend into a paste. Alternatively, pound the ingredients to a paste with a pestle and mortar.

Heat the oil in a large heavy-based frying pan and when hot, but not smoking, add the fennel seeds and fry for a few minutes. Stir in the ginger paste and cook for 2 minutes, stirring frequently. Take care not to burn the mixture.

Reduce the heat, then add the potatoes and cook for 5–7 minutes, stirring frequently, until the potatoes have a golden-brown crust. Add the diced apple and spring onions, then sprinkle with the freshly chopped coriander. Heat through for 2 minutes, then serve on assorted salad leaves with curry-flavoured mayonnaise.

Pizza Pittas

Makes 4

1 tbsp olive oil
1 garlic clove, peeled and crushed
100 g/3½ oz canned chopped tomatoes
2 sun-dried tomatoes, in oil or
rehydrated, chopped
1 tsp dried oregano
pinch unrefined salt
pinch unrefined granulated sugar
4 pitta breads
2 large tomatoes, sliced
100 g/3½ oz grated vegan cheese (look for
a melty, mozzarella-style cheese)
oregano leaves (optional)

Preheat the oven to 200°C/400°F/Gas Mark 6.

Heat the oil in a pan over a medium heat and cook the garlic for 1 minute. Add the chopped and sun-dried tomatoes, oregano, salt and sugar and cook for 10 minutes before blending to make a sauce.

Spread a layer of sauce on top of the pittas. Add the sliced tomato, vegan cheese, and any other desired toppings and cook for 10–15 minutes. Top with oregano and serve.

Japanese Tofu Salad Sandwich

Serves 1

½ tbsp tamari
½ tsp toasted sesame oil
½ tsp maple syrup
1 tsp rice vinegar
2 x 1 cm/½ inch tofu slices
2 tbsp vegetable oil
1 baby leek, sliced lengthways
1 large bread roll, halved
½ tomato, sliced
1 small handful lamb's lettuce
1 large gherkin, sliced
1 tsp sesame seeds

Combine the tamari, sesame oil, maple syrup and vinegar. Add the tofu and coat in the marinade. Leave to stand.

Heat the vegetable oil in a frying pan over a medium heat and fry the leek for 5–10 minutes. Remove from the pan, leaving the oil in the pan. Spread the bread roll with the leftover leek oil.

Fry the tofu in the marinade over a medium heat until the liquid has evaporated, flipping the tofu halfway through cooking. Layer the sandwich with the tomato, tofu, lettuce, gherkin, fried leeks and sesame seeds and serve.

Soups & Stews

Warming, nutritious and bursting with flavour, these soups can be enjoyed as a simple lunch or dinner, or served as a delightful first course to a larger meal. Vegans do not have to sacrifice the indulgent creaminess of the classic Creamy Mushroom Soup, as a vegan version is very easily made. From the rich simplicity of a Borscht to the wholesome heartiness of Cannellini, Kale & Farro Soup, there's a diverse range to choose from.

Rocket & Potato Soup with Garlic Croutons

Serves 4

700 g/1½ lb baby new potatoes
1.1 litres/2 pints vegetable stock
50 g/2 oz rocket leaves
125 g/4 oz thick white sliced bread
50 g/2 oz non-dairy margarine or plant-based buttery spread (*see* page 36)
1 tsp groundnut oil
2–4 garlic cloves, peeled and chopped
125 g/4 oz stale ciabatta bread, with the crusts removed
4 tbsp olive oil
salt and freshly ground black pepper
2 tbsp Parmesan-style vegan cheese, finely grated (optional)

Place the potatoes in a large saucepan, cover with the stock and simmer gently for 10 minutes. Add the rocket leaves and simmer for a further 5–10 minutes until the potatoes are soft and the rocket has wilted.

Meanwhile, make the croûtons. Cut the thick white sliced bread into small cubes and reserve. Heat the margarine or buttery spread and groundnut oil in a small frying pan and cook the garlic for 1 minute, stirring well. Remove the garlic. Add the bread cubes to the margarine and oil mixture in the frying pan and sauté, stirring continuously, until they are golden brown. Drain the croutons on absorbent kitchen paper and reserve.

Cut the ciabatta bread into small dice and stir into the soup. Cover the saucepan and leave to stand for 10 minutes, or until the bread has absorbed a lot of the liquid.

Stir in the olive oil, season to taste with salt and pepper and serve at once with a few of the garlic croutons scattered over the top and a little grated vegan cheese, if using.

Cream of Pumpkin Soup

Serves 4

900 g/2 lb pumpkin flesh (after peeling
and discarding the seeds)
4 tbsp olive oil
1 large onion, peeled
1 leek, trimmed
1 carrot, peeled
2 celery stalks
4 garlic cloves, peeled and crushed
1.7 litres/3 pints water
salt and freshly ground black pepper
¼ tsp freshly grated nutmeg
150 ml/¼ pint vegan single-cream alternative
¼ tsp cayenne pepper
warm herby bread, to serve

Cut the skinned and deseeded pumpkin flesh into 2.5 cm/1 inch cubes. Heat the olive oil in a large saucepan and cook the pumpkin for 2–3 minutes, coating it completely with oil. Chop the onion and leek finely and cut the carrot and celery into small dice.

Add the vegetables to the saucepan with the garlic and cook, stirring, for 5 minutes, or until they have begun to soften. Cover the vegetables with the water and bring to the boil. Season with plenty of salt and pepper and the nutmeg, cover and simmer for 15–20 minutes until all of the vegetables are tender.

When the vegetables are tender, remove from the heat, cool slightly, then pour into a food processor or blender. Liquidise to form a smooth purée, then pass through a sieve into a clean saucepan.

Adjust the seasoning to taste and add all but 2 tablespoons of the vegan cream and enough water to obtain the correct consistency. Bring the soup to boiling point, add the cayenne pepper and serve immediately swirled with vegan cream and warm herby bread.

Mushroom & Sherry Soup

Serves 4

4 slices day-old white bread
zest of ½ lemon
1 tbsp lemon juice
salt and freshly ground black pepper
125 g/4 oz assorted wild mushrooms, lightly rinsed
125 g/4 oz baby button mushrooms, wiped
2 tsp olive oil
1 garlic clove, peeled and crushed
6 spring onions, trimmed and diagonally sliced
600 ml/1 pint vegetable stock
4 tbsp dry sherry
1 tbsp freshly snipped chives, to garnish

Preheat the oven to 180°C/350°F/Gas Mark 4. Remove the crusts from the bread and cut the bread into small cubes.

In a large bowl toss the cubes of bread with the lemon rind and juice, 2 tablespoons of water and plenty of freshly ground black pepper.

Spread the bread cubes on to a lightly oiled, large baking tray and bake for 20 minutes until golden and crisp.

If the wild mushrooms are small, leave some whole. Otherwise, thinly slice all the mushrooms and reserve.

Heat the oil in a saucepan. Add the garlic and spring onions and cook for 1–2 minutes.

Add the mushrooms and cook for 3–4 minutes until they start to soften. Add the vegetable stock and stir to mix.

Bring to the boil, then reduce the heat to a gentle simmer. Cover and cook for 10 minutes.

Stir in the sherry, and season to taste with a little salt and pepper. Pour into warmed bowls, sprinkle over the chives, and serve immediately with the lemon croûtons.

Creamy Mushroom Soup

**Makes 1 large
or 2 smaller bowls**

2 tbsp olive oil
8 chestnut mushrooms, sliced
1 garlic clove, peeled and crushed
1 celery stalk, sliced
1 tbsp soy sauce or tamari
300 ml/10 fl oz unsweetened almond milk
½ tbsp chopped flat-leaf parsley

Heat the oil in a pan and fry the mushrooms, garlic and celery until soft and cooked through.

Blend the soy sauce, milk and cooked vegetables until smooth and creamy. Return the soup to the pan and cook gently until steaming hot but not boiling. Serve topped with parsley.

Borscht

Serves 4

1 medium onion
450 g/1 lb raw beetroot
1.1 litres/2 pints vegetable stock
2 tbsp lemon juice
4 tbsp sherry
salt and freshly ground black pepper

To garnish

4 tbsp vegan yogurt (*see* page 40)
fresh chives, snipped
croutons

Peel the onion, chop finely and place in a large saucepan.

Peel the beetroot if preferred, then grate coarsely. Add the grated beetroot to the large saucepan.

Pour in the stock, bring to the boil and simmer uncovered for 40 minutes. Remove from the heat and allow it to cool slightly before straining into a clean saucepan. Stir in the lemon juice and sherry and adjust the seasoning.

Pour into four soup bowls and add 1 tbsp yogurt to each. Sprinkle with snipped chives and a few croutons. This soup can also be served chilled.

Chunky Vegetable & Fennel Goulash with Dumplings

Serves 4

2 fennel bulbs, weighing about 450 g/1 lb
2 tbsp sunflower oil
1 large onion, peeled and sliced
1½ tbsp paprika
1 tbsp plain flour
300 ml/½ pint vegetable stock
400 g can chopped tomatoes
450 g/1 lb potatoes, peeled and cut into 2.5 cm/1 inch chunks
125 g/4 oz small button mushrooms
salt and freshly ground black pepper

For the dumplings

1 tbsp sunflower oil
1 small onion, peeled and finely chopped
1 portion egg-replacer (*see* page 29)
3 tbsp unsweetened almond or soya milk
3 tbsp freshly chopped parsley
125 g/4 oz fresh white breadcrumbs

Cut the fennel bulbs in half widthways. Thickly slice the stalks and cut the bulbs into eight wedges. Heat the oil in a large saucepan or flameproof casserole dish. Add the onion and fennel and cook gently for 10 minutes until soft. Stir in the paprika and flour.

Remove from the heat and gradually stir in the stock. Add the chopped tomatoes, potatoes and mushrooms. Season to taste with salt and pepper. Bring to the boil, reduce the heat and simmer for 20 minutes.

Meanwhile, make the dumplings. Heat the oil in a frying pan and gently cook the onion for 10 minutes until soft. Leave to cool for a few minutes.

In a bowl, beat the egg-replacer and milk together, then add the onion, parsley and breadcrumbs and season to taste. With damp hands, form the breadcrumb mixture into 12 round dumplings, each about the size of a walnut.

Arrange the dumplings on top of the goulash. Cover and cook for a further 15 minutes until the dumplings are cooked and the vegetables are tender. Serve immediately.

Cannellini, Kale & Farro Soup

Serves 4

100 g/3½ oz farro (if you can't find farro,
use barley groats instead)
2 tbsp olive oil
1 onion, peeled and diced
3 garlic cloves, peeled and crushed
1 rosemary sprig, leaves only
1 carrot, peeled and diced
½ red pepper, diced
2 celery stalks, diced
100 g/3½ oz kale, shredded
200 g/7 oz canned chopped tomatoes
1 litre/1¾ pints water
salt and freshly ground black pepper
200 g/7 oz cooked cannellini beans
125 ml/4 fl oz unsweetened almond milk
crusty bread, to serve

Soak the farro in plenty of room temperature water.

Heat the oil in a pan over a low heat and cook the onion
for 10 minutes. Add the garlic and rosemary and cook for
1 minute. Add the diced vegetables, kale and tomatoes,
cover and sweat over a medium-low heat for 5 minutes.

Add the farro, water and ½ teaspoon salt and bring to the
boil. Reduce the heat, cover and simmer for 20–30 minutes
until the farro is cooked.

Stir in the beans and milk and season. Cook for 10 minutes
until the beans are hot. Serve with bread.

Italian Bean Soup

ℰ

Serves 4

2 tsp olive oil
1 leek, washed and chopped
1 garlic clove, peeled and crushed
2 tsp dried oregano
75 g/3 oz green beans, trimmed and cut
into bite-size pieces
410 g can cannellini beans,
drained and rinsed
75 g/3 oz small pasta shapes
1 litre/1¾ pint vegetable stock
8 cherry tomatoes
salt and freshly ground black pepper
3 tbsp freshly shredded basil

Heat the oil in a large saucepan. Add the leek, garlic and oregano and cook gently for 5 minutes, stirring occasionally.

Stir in the green beans and the cannellini beans. Sprinkle in the pasta and pour in the stock.

Bring the stock mixture to the boil, then reduce the heat to a simmer.

Cook for 12–15 minutes or until the vegetables are tender and the pasta is cooked to al dente. Stir occasionally.

In a heavy-based frying pan, dry-fry the tomatoes over a high heat until they soften and the skins begin to blacken.

Gently crush the tomatoes in the pan with the back of a spoon and add to the soup.

Season to taste with salt and pepper. Stir in the shredded basil and serve immediately.

Carrot & Ginger Soup

Serves 4

4 slices of bread, crusts removed
1 tsp yeast extract
2 tsp olive oil
1 onion, peeled and chopped
1 garlic clove, peeled and crushed
½ tsp ground ginger
450 g/1 lb carrots, peeled and chopped
1 litre/1¾ pint vegetable stock
2.5 cm/1 inch piece of root ginger, peeled
and finely grated
salt and freshly ground black pepper
1 tbsp lemon juice

To garnish

chives
lemon zest

Preheat the oven to 180°C/350°F/Gas Mark 4. Roughly chop the bread. Dissolve the yeast extract in 2 tablespoons of warm water and mix with the bread.

Spread the bread cubes over a lightly oiled baking tray and bake for 20 minutes, turning half way through. Remove from the oven and reserve.

Heat the oil in a large saucepan. Gently cook the onion and garlic for 3–4 minutes.

Stir in the ground ginger and cook for 1 minute to release the flavour.

Add the chopped carrots, then stir in the stock and the fresh ginger. Simmer gently for 15 minutes.

Remove from the heat and allow to cool a little. Blend until smooth, then season to taste with salt and pepper. Stir in the lemon juice. Garnish with the chives and lemon zest and serve immediately.

Bread & Tomato Soup

Serves 4

900 g/2 lb very ripe tomatoes
4 tbsp olive oil
1 onion, peeled and finely chopped
1 tbsp freshly chopped basil
3 garlic cloves, peeled and crushed
¼ tsp hot chilli powder
salt and freshly ground black pepper
600 ml/1 pint vegetable stock
175 g/6 oz stale white bread
50 g/2 oz cucumber, cut into small dice
4 whole basil leaves

Make a small cross in the base of each tomato, then place in a bowl and cover with boiling water. Allow to stand for 2 minutes, or until the skins have started to peel away, then drain, remove the skins and seeds and chop into large pieces.

Heat 3 tablespoons of the olive oil in a saucepan and gently cook the onion until softened. Add the skinned tomatoes, chopped basil, garlic and chilli powder and season to taste with salt and pepper. Pour in the stock, cover the saucepan, bring to the boil and simmer gently for 15–20 minutes.

Remove the crusts from the bread and break into small pieces. Remove the tomato mixture from the heat and stir in the bread. Cover and leave to stand for 10 minutes, or until the bread has blended with the tomatoes. Season to taste. Serve warm or cold with a swirl of olive oil on the top, garnished with a spoonful of chopped cucumber and basil leaves.

Salads

Salads may be an obvious choice for a vegan – but while they are only one of many options, it would be foolish to ignore this most versatile, healthy and natural dish of the vegan repertoire. However, many salads contain hidden animal products such as dairy, honey or anchovies in dressings, or sneaky cubes of cheese or meat. So here are our top picks for a range of delicious vegan-safe salads, from Asian-inspired Crispy Noodle Salad to the sunny vibe of Sicilian Baked Aubergine Salad.

Cold Sesame Noodles

Serves 4-8

450 g/1 lb soba noodles or wholewheat
spaghetti
salt
1 tbsp sesame oil
1 tbsp groundnut oil
1 green pepper, deseeded and thinly sliced
125 g/4 oz daikon, cut into
julienne strips
125 g/4 oz mangetout or green beans,
trimmed and sliced
2 garlic cloves, peeled and finely chopped
2 tbsp soy sauce, or to taste
1 tbsp cider vinegar
2 tbsp sweet chilli sauce, or to taste
2 tsp sugar
75 g/3 oz peanut butter
6-8 spring onions, trimmed and
diagonally sliced

To garnish

Toasted sesame seeds
Julienne strips of cucumber

Bring a large pan of lightly salted water to a rolling boil. Add the noodles or spaghetti and cook according to the packet instructions, or until *al dente*. Drain, rinse and drain again, then toss in the sesame oil and reserve.

Heat the groundnut oil in a wok or large frying pan over a high heat. Add the green pepper, daikon and mangetout or green beans and stir-fry for 1 minute. Stir in the garlic and cook for 30 seconds.

Add the soy sauce to the pan with the vinegar, chilli sauce, sugar, peanut butter and 50 ml/2 fl oz of hot water. Simmer, stirring constantly, until the peanut butter is smooth, adding a little more water if necessary and adjusting the seasoning to taste.

Add the spring onions and the reserved noodles or spaghetti to the peanut sauce and cook, stirring, for 2–3 minutes, or until heated through. Tip the mixture into a large serving bowl and allow to cool to room temperature, stirring occasionally. Garnish with the toasted sesame seeds and cucumber julienne strips before serving.

Food Fact: Daikon, also known as mooli or white radish, resembles a parsnip in shape. It has a very fresh, peppery flavour and is often used in salads either peeled or grated. Because it has a high water content, it should be sprinkled with salt and allowed to drain in a sieve over a bowl for about 30 minutes after preparing. Rinse well under cold running water and pat dry on absorbent kitchen paper before stir-frying.

Crispy Noodle Salad

Serves 4-8

2 tbsp sunflower seeds
2 tbsp pumpkin seeds
50 g/2 oz rice vermicelli or stir-fry noodles
175 g/6 oz non-dairy margarine
2 tbsp sesame seeds, lightly toasted
125 g/4 oz red cabbage, trimmed
and shredded
1 orange pepper, deseeded and
finely chopped
125 g/4 oz button mushrooms, wiped
and quartered
2 spring onions, trimmed and
finely chopped
salt and freshly ground black pepper
shredded pickled sushi ginger, to garnish

Preheat the oven to 200°C/400°F/Gas Mark 6, then sprinkle the sunflower and pumpkin seeds on a baking sheet. Toast in the oven, stirring occasionally, for 10–15 minutes or until lightly toasted. Remove from the oven and leave to cool.

Crush the rice vermicelli into small pieces (this is easiest in a plastic bag or while the noodles are still in the packet), and reserve. Melt the margarine in a small saucepan and leave to cool for a few minutes. Pour the clear yellow liquid carefully into a bowl, leaving behind the white milky solids. Discard the milky solids.

Heat the yellow, clarified margarine in a wok and fry the crushed noodles in batches until browned, stirring constantly and gently. Remove the fried noodles as they cook, using a slotted spoon, and drain on absorbent kitchen paper. Transfer the noodles to a bowl and add the toasted seeds.

Mix together the red cabbage, orange pepper, button mushrooms and spring onions in a large bowl and season to taste with salt and pepper. Just before serving, add the noodles and seeds to the salad and mix gently. Garnish with a little sushi ginger and serve.

Warm Leek & Tomato Salad

Serves 4

450 g/1 lb trimmed baby leeks
225 g/8 oz ripe, but firm tomatoes
2 shallots, peeled and cut into thin wedges

For the honey and lime dressing

2 tbsp clear honey
grated rind of 1 lime
4 tbsp lime juice
1 tbsp light olive oil
1 tsp Dijon mustard
salt and freshly ground black pepper

To garnish

freshly chopped tarragon
freshly chopped basil

Trim the leeks so that they are all the same length. Place in a steamer over a pan of boiling water and steam for 8 minutes or until just tender.

Drain the leeks thoroughly and arrange in a shallow serving dish.

Make a cross in the top of the tomatoes, place in a bowl and cover them with boiling water until their skins start to peel away. Remove from the bowl and carefully remove the skins.

Cut the tomatoes into 4 and remove the seeds, then chop into small dice. Spoon over the top of the leeks together with the shallots.

In a small bowl make the dressing by whisking the honey, lime rind, lime juice, olive oil, mustard and salt and pepper. Pour 3 tablespoons of the dressing over the leeks and tomatoes and garnish with the tarragon and basil. Serve while the leeks are still warm, with the remaining dressing served separately.

Bulghur Wheat Salad with Minty Lemon Dressing

Serves 4

125 g/4 oz bulghur wheat
10 cm/4 inch piece cucumber
2 shallots, peeled
125 g/4 oz baby sweetcorn
3 ripe but firm tomatoes

For the dressing
grated rind of 1 lemon
3 tbsp lemon juice
3 tbsp freshly chopped mint
2 tbsp freshly chopped parsley
1–2 tsp agave nector or other vegan sweetener
2 tbsp sunflower oil
salt and freshly ground black pepper

Place the bulghur wheat in a saucepan and cover with boiling water.

Simmer for about 10 minutes, then drain thoroughly and turn into a serving bowl.

Cut the cucumber into small dice, chop the shallots finely and reserve. Steam the sweetcorn over a pan of boiling water for 10 minutes or until tender. Drain and slice into thick chunks.

Cut a cross on the top of each tomato and place in boiling water until their skins start to peel away.

Remove the skins and the seeds and cut the tomatoes into small dice.

Make the dressing by briskly whisking all the ingredients in a small bowl until mixed well. When the bulghur wheat has cooled a little, add all the prepared vegetables and stir in the dressing. Season to taste with salt and pepper and serve.

Sicilian Baked Aubergine Salad

Serves 4

1 large aubergine, trimmed
2 celery stalks, trimmed
4 large ripe tomatoes
1 tsp sunflower oil
2 shallots, peeled and finely chopped
1½ tsp tomato purée
25 g/1 oz green pitted olives
25 g/1 oz black pitted olives
salt and freshly ground black pepper
1 tbsp white wine vinegar
2 tsp caster sugar
1 tbsp freshly chopped basil, to garnish
mixed salad leaves, to serve

Preheat the oven to 200°C/400°F/Gas Mark 6. Cut the aubergine into small cubes and place on an oiled baking tray.

Cover the tray with tinfoil and bake in the preheated oven for 15–20 minutes until soft. Reserve, to allow the aubergine to cool.

Place the celery and tomatoes in a large bowl and cover with boiling water.

Remove the tomatoes from the bowl when their skins begin to peel away. Remove the skins then, deseed and chop the flesh into small pieces.

Remove the celery from the bowl of water, finely chop and reserve.

Pour the vegetable oil into a non-stick saucepan, add the chopped shallots and fry gently for 2–3 minutes until soft. Add the celery, tomatoes, tomato purée and olives. Season to taste with salt and pepper.

Simmer gently for 3–4 minutes. Add the vinegar, sugar and cooled aubergine to the pan and heat gently for 2–3 minutes until all the ingredients are well blended. Reserve to allow the aubergine mixture to cool. When cool, garnish with the chopped basil and serve cold with salad leaves.

Chinese Salad with Soy & Ginger Dressing

Serves 4

1 head of Chinese cabbage
200 g can water chestnuts, drained
6 spring onions, trimmed
4 ripe but firm cherry tomatoes
125 g/4 oz mangetout
125 g/4 oz beansprouts
2 tbsp freshly chopped coriander

Soy and Ginger Dressing:

2 tbsp sunflower oil
4 tbsp light soy sauce
2.5 cm/1 inch piece root ginger, peeled and finely grated
zest and juice of 1 lemon
salt and freshly ground black pepper
crusty white bread, to serve

Rinse and finely shred the Chinese cabbage and place in a serving dish.

Slice the water chestnuts into small slivers and cut the spring onions diagonally into 2.5 cm/1 inch lengths, then split lengthwise into thin strips.

Cut the tomatoes in half and then slice each half into 3 wedges and reserve.

Simmer the mangetout in boiling water for 2 minutes until beginning to soften, drain and cut in half diagonally.

Arrange the water chestnuts, spring onions, mangetout, tomatoes and beansprouts on top of the shredded Chinese cabbage. Garnish with the freshly chopped coriander.

Make the dressing by whisking all the ingredients together in a small bowl until mixed thoroughly. Serve with the bread and the salad.

Fishless Tuna Pasta Salad

Serves 4

400 g/14 oz canned chickpeas
56 g/2¼ oz vegan mayonnaise
1 tbsp Dijon mustard
1½ tbsp red wine vinegar
large pinch salt
100 g/3½ oz macaroni pasta
2 gherkins (pickles), sliced
2 tbsp olive oil
1 tbsp lemon juice
salt and freshly ground black pepper
1 tbsp chopped chives,
for topping (optional)

Pulse the chickpeas in a food processor 2 or 3 times. Stir in the mayonnaise, mustard, vinegar and salt. Set aside.

Cook the macaroni in a pan according to the packet instructions. Drain and refresh in cold water. Combine the pasta with the gherkins (pickles), oil and lemon juice. Stir through the chickpea mix and season.

Top with chives, if liked.

Panzanella

Serves 4

250 g/9 oz day-old Italian-style bread
1 tbsp red wine vinegar
4 tbsp olive oil
1 tsp lemon juice
1 small garlic clove, peeled and
finely chopped
1 red onion, peeled and finely sliced
1 cucumber, peeled if preferred
225 g/8 oz ripe tomatoes, deseeded
150 g/5 oz pitted black olives
about 20 basil leaves, coarsely torn,
or left whole if small
sea salt and freshly ground black pepper

Cut the bread into thick slices, leaving the crusts on. Add 1 teaspoon of the red wine vinegar to a jug of iced water, put the slices of bread in a bowl and pour over the water. Make sure the bread is covered completely. Leave to soak for 3–4 minutes until just soft.

Remove the soaked bread from the water and squeeze it gently, first with your hands and then in a clean tea towel to remove any excess water. Put the bread on a plate, cover with clingfilm and chill in the refrigerator for about 1 hour.

Meanwhile, whisk together the olive oil, the remaining red wine vinegar and lemon juice in a large serving bowl. Add the garlic and onion and stir to coat well.

Halve the cucumber and remove the seeds. Chop both the cucumber and tomatoes into 1 cm/½ inch dice. Add to the garlic and onion with the olives. Tear the bread into bite-size chunks and add to the bowl with the fresh basil leaves. Toss together to mix and serve immediately with a grinding of sea salt and black pepper.

Potato & Runner Bean Salad

**Serves 2 as a main dish
or 4 as a starter**

450 g/1 lb (16 oz) potatoes, peeled
300 g/11 oz runner beans, cut into
generous chunks

For the dressing
3 tbsp olive oil
2 bird's-eye (Thai) chilies (peppers),
deseeded and cut into fat slices
1 shallot, peeled and sliced
1 rosemary sprig
pinch unrefined salt

Cook the potatoes in a pan of boiling water for 20 minutes until still firm but a knife pierces them easily. Drain, refresh in cold water and set aside.

Steam the beans for 10 minutes until tender, then refresh in cold water and set aside.

For the dressing, heat the oil in a pan over a medium heat and fry the remaining ingredients for 10 minutes until the shallot is soft.

Meanwhile, cut the potatoes into slices. Carefully combine the potato slices, beans and dressing and serve on a large plate.

Beetroot & Potato Medley

Serves 4

350 g/12 oz raw baby beetroot
½ tsp sunflower oil
225 g/8 oz new potatoes
½ cucumber, peeled
3 tbsp white wine vinegar
150 ml/5 fl oz vegan yogurt (*see* page 40)
salt and freshly ground black pepper
fresh salad leaves
1 tbsp freshly snipped chives, to garnish

Preheat the oven to 180°C/350°F/Gas Mark 4. Scrub the beetroot thoroughly and place on a baking tray.

Brush the beetroot with a little oil and cook for 1½ hours or until a skewer is easily insertable into the beetroot. Allow to cool a little, then remove the skins.

Cook the potatoes in boiling water for about 10 minutes. Rinse in cold water and drain. Reserve the potatoes until cool. Dice evenly.

Cut the cucumber into cubes and place in a mixing bowl. Chop the beetroot into small cubes and add to the bowl with the reserved potatoes. Gently mix the vegetables together.

Mix together the vinegar and yogurt and season to taste with a little salt and pepper. Pour over the vegetables and combine gently.

Arrange on a bed of salad leaves garnished with the snipped chives and serve.

Carrot, Celeriac & Sesame Seed Salad

Serves 6

225 g/8 oz celeriac
225 g/8 oz carrots, peeled
50 g/2 oz seedless raisins
2 tbsp sesame seeds
freshly chopped parsley, to garnish

For the lemon and chilli dressing

grated rind of 1 lemon
4 tbsp lemon juice
2 tbsp sunflower oil
2 tbsp clear honey
1 red bird's eye chilli, deseeded and
finely chopped
salt and freshly ground black pepper

Slice the celeriac into thin matchsticks. Place in a small saucepan of boiling salted water and boil for 2 minutes.

Drain and rinse the celeriac in cold water and place in a mixing bowl.

Finely grate the carrot. Add the carrot and the raisins to the celeriac in the bowl.

Place the sesame seeds under a hot grill or dry-fry in a frying pan for 1–2 minutes until golden brown, then leave to cool.

Make the dressing by whisking together the lemon rind, lemon juice, oil, honey, chilli and seasoning or by shaking thoroughly in a screw-topped jar.

Pour 2 tablespoons of the dressing over the salad and toss well. Turn into a serving dish and sprinkle over the toasted sesame seeds and chopped parsley. Serve the remaining dressing separately.

Hearty Mains

Vegan food can be just as filling and satisfying as the meatiest of fare. This section provides a tantalising selection of recipes for your supper or family meal, from a virtuous Three Bean Tagine to the warming and comforting Italian Bake. If you miss a Sunday Roast why not try the Vegan Nut Roast, and if you yearn for the indulgence of a burger of the ooziness of cheese, our Best Veggie Burger Ever and Cauliflower Mac 'n' Cheeze will be sure to hit the spot.

Vegan Nut Roast

Serves 4

1 tbsp vegetable oil, plus extra for oiling
1 large onion, peeled and diced
1 tsp ground cumin
100 ml/3½ fl oz boiling water
1 vegan stock cube
1 heaped tsp yeast extract
225 g/8 oz mixed nuts, including the brazil
nuts, finely chopped
40 g/1½ oz grated carrot
100 g/3½ oz wholemeal bread,
blitzed into breadcrumbs
salt and freshly ground black pepper

Preheat the oven to 180°C/350°F/Gas Mark 4. Oil a 450-g/1-lb loaf tin.

Heat the oil in a frying pan over a low heat and cook the onions and cumin for 10 minutes until the onions are translucent.

Mix the boiling water with the stock cube and yeast extract in a heatproof jug. Add to the pan and bring to the boil.

Mix the chopped nuts, grated carrot and breadcrumbs together in a large bowl. Add the stock to make a mixture that is sticky but not wet. If the mixture doesn't stick together, add 1 tablespoon boiling water at a time until it holds together. Season to taste. Press and flatten firmly into the tin and bake for 25–35 minutes until browned on top. Serve.

Three Bean Tagine

Serves 4

few saffron strands
2–3 tbsp olive oil
1 small aubergine, trimmed and diced
1 onion, peeled and chopped
350 g/12 oz sweet potatoes,
peeled and diced
225 g/8 oz carrots, peeled and chopped
1 cinnamon stick, bruised
1½ tsp ground cumin
salt and freshly ground black pepper
600 ml/1 pint vegetable stock
2 fresh mint sprigs
200 g/7 oz canned red kidney beans, drained
300 g/11 oz canned haricot beans, drained
300 g/11 oz canned flageolet beans, drained
125 g/4 oz ready-to-eat dried
apricots, chopped
1 tbsp freshly chopped mint, to garnish

Place warm water into a small bowl and sprinkle with saffron strands. Leave to infuse for at least 10 minutes.

Heat the oil in a large heavy-based saucepan, add the aubergine and onion and sauté for 5 minutes before adding the sweet potato, carrots, cinnamon stick and ground cumin. Cook, stirring, until the vegetables are lightly coated in the cumin. Add the saffron with the soaking liquid and season to taste with salt and pepper. Pour in the stock and add the mint sprigs.

Rinse the beans, add to the pan and bring to the boil. Reduce the heat, cover with a lid and simmer for 20 minutes. Add the apricots and cook, stirring occasionally, for a further 10 minutes, or until the vegetables are tender. Adjust the seasoning to taste, then serve sprinkled with chopped mint.

Spaghetti Puttanesca

Serves 2

165 g/5½ oz spaghetti
3 tbsp olive oil
2 garlic cloves, peeled and crushed
½ tsp chili flakes
50 g/2 oz pitted mixed olives
1½ tbsp rinsed capers
1 tsp dried oregano
300 g/11 oz canned chopped tomatoes
2 tbsp tomato purée
salt and freshly ground black pepper

To serve
green salad
crusty bread

Cook the spaghetti according to the packet instructions.

Meanwhile, heat the oil in a large frying pan over a medium-low heat and fry the garlic, chili flakes, olives, capers and oregano for 2 minutes. Add the tomatoes and tomato purée and bring to the boil. Reduce the heat and simmer until the pasta is ready.

Drain the pasta and return it to the pan. Season the sauce, then add half the sauce, mostly without olives, to the pasta and mix it through. Divide among bowls, top with the remaining sauce and serve with a green salad and bread.

Vegetable Cassoulet

Serves 6

2 tbsp olive oil

2 garlic cloves, peeled and chopped

225 g/8 oz baby onions, peeled and halved

150 g/5 oz carrots, peeled and diced

2 celery sticks, trimmed and finely chopped

1 red pepper, deseeded and chopped

175 g/6 oz mixed mushrooms,
wiped and sliced

1 tbsp each freshly chopped rosemary,
thyme and sage

150 ml/¼ pint vegan red wine

400 g/14 oz can haricot beans,
drained and rinsed

4 tbsp tomato purée

1 tbsp dark soy sauce

salt and freshly ground black pepper

50 g/2 oz fresh breadcrumbs

1 tbsp freshly chopped parsley

basil sprigs, to garnish

Preheat the oven to 190°C/375°F/Gas Mark 5. Heat 1 tablespoon of the oil in an ovenproof casserole and add the garlic, onions, carrots, celery and red pepper. Cook gently for 10–12 minutes, until tender and starting to brown. Add a little water if the vegetables start to stick. Add the mushrooms and cook for a further 5 minutes, until softened. Add the herbs and stir briefly.

Stir in the red wine and boil rapidly for about 5 minutes, until reduced and syrupy. Stir in the haricot beans, tomato purée and soy sauce. Season to taste with salt and pepper.

Mix together the breadcrumbs and parsley with the remaining 1 tablespoon of oil. Scatter this mixture evenly over the top of the cassoulet. Cover loosely with foil and transfer to the preheated oven. Cook for 30 minutes. Carefully remove the foil and cook for a further 15–20 minutes, until the topping is crisp and golden. Serve immediately, garnished with basil sprigs.

Vegetable & Lentil Casserole

Serves 4

225 g/8 oz Puy lentils
1–2 tbsp olive oil
1 onion, peeled and chopped
2–3 garlic cloves, peeled and crushed
300 g/11 oz carrots, peeled and
cut into chunks
3 celery stalks, trimmed and sliced
350 g/12 oz butternut squash, peeled,
deseeded and diced
1 litre/1¾ pints vegetable stock
salt and freshly ground black pepper
few fresh oregano sprigs, plus extra
to garnish
1 large red pepper, deseeded and chopped
2 courgettes, trimmed and sliced
150 ml/¼ pint vegan yogurt, to serve
(*see* page 40)

Preheat the oven to 160°C/325°F/Gas Mark 3. Pour the lentils out onto a plate and look through them for any small stones, then rinse the lentils and reserve.

Heat the oil in a large ovenproof casserole dish (or a deep frying pan, if preferred), add the onion, garlic, carrots and celery and sauté for 5 minutes, stirring occasionally.

Add the squash and lentils. Pour in the stock and season to taste with salt and pepper.

Add the oregano sprigs and bring to the boil.

If a frying pan has been used, transfer everything to a casserole dish. Cover with a lid and cook in the oven for 25 minutes.

Remove the casserole from the oven, add the red pepper and courgettes and stir. Return the casserole to the oven and cook for a further 20 minutes, or until all the vegetables are tender. Adjust the seasoning, garnish with sprigs of oregano and serve with yogurt on the side.

Spinach & Mushroom Pancakes with Béchamel Sauce

❦

Serves 2

For the filling

200 g/7 oz spinach
1 tbsp olive oil
1 onion, peeled and diced
2 garlic cloves, peeled and crushed
200 g/7 oz chestnut mushrooms, sliced
¼ tsp salt

For the sauce

300 ml/10 fl oz unsweetened soya milk
2 tbsp vegetable oil
2 tbsp plain flour
salt and freshly ground black pepper

For the pancakes

50 g/2 oz plain flour
1 tbsp ground flaxseed
150 ml/5 fl oz unsweetened soya milk
2 tsp vegetable oil
pinch salt

Steam the spinach for 5 minutes. Set a small handful of spinach aside, squeezing the rest to remove excess liquid. Heat the oil in a pan and sauté the onion for 10 minutes until translucent. Add the garlic and cook for 1 minute, then add the mushrooms and salt and cook until soft. Keep warm.

For the sauce, gently scald the milk in a pan without boiling. Mix the oil and flour together in a small pan and cook for 2 minutes, stirring. Remove from the heat and mix in the hot milk. Bring the sauce to the boil, stirring. Reduce the heat and simmer for 2 minutes. Season.

Blend the pancake ingredients until smooth, then cook the pancakes according to the recipe on page 88.

Preheat the grill to medium. Spoon some of the filling along the centre of each pancake, roll up and place in a small ovenproof dish. Top with the remaining spinach and sauce and grill for a few minutes until browned.

Note: You can make each of the three recipes in advance, freezing the pancakes and the filling to save time. Serve with a simple green salad.

Sweet Potato Cakes with Mango & Tomato Salsa

Serves 4

700 g/1½ lb sweet potatoes, peeled and cut into large chunks
25 g/1 oz non-dairy margarine or plant-based buttery spread (*see* page 36)
1 onion, peeled and chopped
1 garlic clove, peeled and crushed
pinch freshly grated nutmeg
salt and freshly ground black pepper
1 portion egg-replacer, beaten (*see* page 29)
50 g/2 oz quick-cook polenta
2 tbsp sunflower oil

For the salsa

1 ripe mango, peeled, stoned and diced
6 cherry tomatoes, cut into wedges
4 spring onions, trimmed and thinly sliced
1 red chilli, deseeded and finely chopped
finely grated zest and juice of ½ lime
2 tbsp freshly chopped mint
1 tsp clear honey
salad leaves, to serve

Steam or cook the sweet potatoes in lightly salted boiling water for 15–20 minutes until tender. Drain well, then mash until smooth.

Melt the margarine or buttery spread in a saucepan. Add the onion and garlic and cook gently for 10 minutes until soft. Add to the mashed sweet potato and season with the nutmeg, salt and pepper. Stir together until mixed thoroughly. Leave to cool.

Shape the mixture into four oval potato cakes, about 2.5 cm/1 inch thick. Dip first in the beaten egg-replacer, allowing the excess to fall back into the bowl, then coat in the polenta. Refrigerate for at least 30 minutes.

Meanwhile, mix together all the ingredients for the salsa. Spoon into a serving bowl, cover with clingfilm and leave at room temperature to allow the flavours to develop.

Heat the oil in a frying pan and cook the potato cakes for 4–5 minutes on each side. Serve with the salsa and salad leaves.

Lentil Tacos

Serves 2

2 tbsp vegetable oil
1 onion, peeled and diced
2 garlic cloves, peeled and crushed
1 tsp ground cumin
1 tsp ground coriander
½ tsp mild chili powder
250 g/9 oz cooked green lentils
50 g/2 oz cooked kidney beans
¼ tsp unrefined salt
4 taco shells
coriander leaves, for sprinkling

Heat the oil in a pan and fry the onion until soft. Add the garlic and spices and cook for 1 minute.

Stir in the lentils, beans and salt and cook over a medium heat for 5 minutes until the beans are hot.

Spoon the mixture into tacos and top with coriander. Serve these lovely tacos with guacamole and Pico de Gallo (*see* page 82) for a comforting lunch or relaxed supper.

Chili & Rice

Serves 2

3 tbsp olive oil
1 onion, peeled and diced
6 mushrooms, sliced
1 red pepper, cored, deseeded
and diced
2 garlic cloves, peeled and crushed
½ tsp medium-hot chili powder
1 tsp smoked paprika
1 tsp ground cumin
2 tsp dried oregano
400 g/14 oz canned chopped tomatoes
200 g/7 oz cooked red kidney beans
1 tbsp lime juice
pinch unrefined granulated sugar
¼ tsp unrefined salt
150 g/5 oz/generous white rice
vegan yogurt, to serve (*see* page 40)

Heat the oil in a pan over a medium heat and cook the onion for 5 minutes. Add the mushrooms and pepper and cook for 5 minutes. Mix in the garlic, spices and oregano and cook for 1 minute. Add the canned tomatoes, beans, lime juice, sugar and salt, bring to the boil, reduce the heat and simmer, uncovered, for 20 minutes.

Cook the rice according to the packet instructions.

Serve the rice topped with chili, and a dollop of vegan yogurt on top, if liked.

Best Veggie Burger Ever

Makes 2

For the herb salsa
3 tbsp chopped parsley
3 tbsp chopped oregano
1 tbsp olive oil
2 tsp lemon juice
large pinch salt

For the burgers
3 tbsp olive oil
2 garlic cloves, peeled and crushed
1 tsp ground cumin
1 tsp smoked paprika
300 g/11 oz cooked chickpeas, mashed
1 tbsp ground flaxseed
¼ tsp salt

For the best veggie burger ever!
2 ciabatta buns, or your favourite burger bun
2 tbsp vegan mayonnaise
1 handful baby spinach
6 cucumber slices
1 handful alfalfa sprouts
½ avocado, sliced

For the salsa, mix all the ingredients together and set aside.

For the burgers, heat 1 tablespoon of the oil in a frying pan and fry the garlic and spices for 1 minute. Stir in the chickpeas with the ground flaxseed and salt, then roughly mix in 4 tablespoons of the salsa. Make 2 patties and fry them in the remaining oil for 5 minutes on each side until browned.

Cut the rolls in half and spread with mayonnaise and the remaining salsa. Add spinach, cucumber, alfalfa sprouts, avocado and a burger and serve.

Vegetable Bake

Serves 4

300 g/11 oz broccoli florets, trimmed

450 g/1 lb old-season (baking) potatoes, peeled

2 tbsp olive oil

8 baby onions, peeled, and halved if large

225 g/8 oz carrots, peeled and cut into small chunks

1 red pepper, deseeded and sliced

1 yellow pepper, deseeded and sliced

400 g can black-eye beans, drained, rinsed and drained again

600 ml/1 pint vegetable stock

1½ tbsp cornflour

2 tbsp cold water

salt and freshly ground black pepper

2 tbsp fresh mixed herbs, chopped

1 tbsp non-dairy margarine or plant-based buttery spread (*see* page 36), if desired

25 g/1 oz vegan cheese, grated

Preheat the oven to 180°C/350°F/Gas Mark 4, 10 minutes before required. Plunge the broccoli into boiling water. Leave for 5 minutes, then drain and reserve. Coarsely grate the potatoes and cover with cold water. Leave for 10–15 minutes, drain and re-cover with cold water until required.

Heat the oil in a large saucepan or frying pan over a low heat. Add the onions and carrots and fry for 10 minutes, or until beginning to soften. Add the peppers and fry for a further 5 minutes. Remove from the heat and stir in the broccoli. Place in a 1.1 litre/2 pint ovenproof dish. Stir in the drained beans and reserve.

Pour the stock into a clean pan and bring to the boil. Blend the cornflour to a smooth paste with the 2 tbsp of cold water. Stir into the stock and cook, stirring continuously, until the mixture thickens. Season to taste and add the chopped herbs, then pour the sauce over the vegetables.

Drain the grated potatoes well and place them on top, ensuring all the vegetables are covered. Dot with the margarine or buttery spread, if using, then sprinkle with the grated cheese. Place the dish on a baking sheet and cook in the preheated oven for 30 minutes, or until the vegetables are tender and the top is golden. Serve immediately.

Italian Bake

Serves 4

Preheat the oven to 180°C/350°F/Gas Mark 4.

For the topping

6 slices stale bread
1 tbsp thyme leaves
¼ tsp unrefined salt
1 tbsp olive oil
1 tsp lemon zest
1 tbsp lemon juice

For the topping, blitz all the ingredients together in a food processor until the bread becomes breadcrumbs. Set aside.

Combine all the remaining ingredients in an ovenproof dish and roast for 15 minutes. Remove from the oven and turn the vegetables. Top with the breadcrumb mixture and cook for 30 minutes until browned and crispy. Serve with salad.

For the vegetables

2 tbsp olive oil
1 medium onion, peeled and diced
4 garlic cloves, peeled and crushed
1 tbsp dried oregano
1 tbsp dried or fresh rosemary
¼ tsp salt
pinch unrefined granulated sugar
900 g/2 lb cherry tomatoes
1 orange pepper, cored, deseeded and diced
green salad, to serve

Pasta with Walnut Sauce

Serves 4

50 g/2 oz walnuts, toasted
3 spring onions, trimmed and chopped
2 garlic cloves, peeled and sliced
1 tbsp freshly chopped parsley or basil
5 tbsp extra virgin olive oil
salt and freshly ground black pepper
450 g/1 lb broccoli, cut into florets
350 g/12 oz pasta shapes
1 red chilli, deseeded and finely chopped

Place the toasted walnuts in a blender or food processor with the chopped spring onions, one of the garlic cloves and parsley or basil. Blend to a fairly smooth paste, then gradually add 3 tablespoons of the olive oil, until it is well mixed into the paste. Season the walnut paste to taste with salt and pepper and reserve.

Bring a large pan of lightly salted water to a rolling boil. Add the broccoli, return to the boil and cook for 2 minutes. Remove the broccoli, using a slotted draining spoon and refresh under cold running water. Drain again and pat dry on absorbent kitchen paper.

Bring the water back to a rolling boil. Add the pasta and cook according to the packet instructions, or until *al dente*.

Meanwhile, heat the remaining oil in a frying pan. Add the remaining garlic and chilli. Cook gently for 2 minutes, or until softened. Add the broccoli and walnut paste. Cook for a further 3–4 minutes, or until heated through.

Drain the pasta thoroughly and transfer to a large warmed serving bowl. Pour over the walnut and broccoli sauce. Toss together, adjust the seasoning and serve immediately.

Tiny Pasta with Fresh Herb Sauce

Serves 6

375 g/13 oz tripolini (small bows with
rounded ends) or small farfalle
2 tbsp freshly chopped flat-leaf parsley
2 tbsp freshly chopped basil
1 tbsp freshly snipped chives
1 tbsp freshly chopped chervil
1 tbsp freshly chopped tarragon
1 tbsp freshly chopped sage
1 tbsp freshly chopped oregano
1 tbsp freshly chopped marjoram
1 tbsp freshly chopped thyme
1 tbsp freshly chopped rosemary
finely grated zest of 1 lemon
75 ml/3 fl oz extra virgin olive oil
2 garlic cloves, peeled and finely chopped
½ tsp dried chilli flakes
salt and freshly ground black pepper
freshly grated Parmesan-style vegan
cheese, to serve

Bring a large pan of lightly salted water to a rolling boil. Add
the pasta and cook according to the packet instructions, or
until *al dente*.

Meanwhile, place all the herbs, the lemon zest, olive oil,
garlic and chilli flakes in a heavy-based pan. Heat gently
for 2–3 minutes, or until the herbs turn bright green and
become very fragrant. Remove from the heat and season to
taste with salt and pepper.

Drain the pasta thoroughly, reserving 2–3 tablespoons of the
cooking water. Transfer the pasta to a large warmed bowl.

Pour the heated herb mixture over the pasta and toss
together until thoroughly mixed. Check and adjust the
seasoning, adding a little of the pasta cooking water if the
pasta mixture seems a bit dry. Transfer to warmed serving
dishes and serve immediately with grated cheese.

Rigatoni with Roasted Beetroot & Rocket

Serves 4

350 g/12 oz raw baby beetroot, unpeeled
1 garlic clove, peeled and crushed
½ tsp finely grated orange rind
1 tbsp orange juice
1 tsp lemon juice
2 tbsp walnut oil
salt and freshly ground black pepper
350 g/12 oz dried fettucini
75 g/3 oz rocket leaves
125 g/4 oz vegan blue cheese, cut into
small cubes (optional)

Preheat oven to 150°C/300°F/Gas Mark 2, 10 minutes before cooking. Wrap the beetroot individually in tinfoil and bake for 1–1½ hours, or until tender. (Test by opening one of the parcels and scraping the skin away from the stem end – it should come off very easily.)

Leave the beetroot until cool enough to handle, then peel and cut each beetroot into 6–8 wedges, depending on the size. Mix the garlic, orange rind and juice, lemon juice, walnut oil and salt and pepper together, then drizzle over the beetroot and toss to coat well.

Meanwhile, bring a large saucepan of lightly salted water to the boil. Cook the pasta for 10 minutes, or until *al dente*.

Drain the pasta thoroughly, then add the warm beetroot, rocket leaves and vegan blue cheese, if using. Quickly and gently toss together, then divide between serving bowls and serve immediately before the rocket wilts.

Spaghetti with Meatless Balls

Serves 2

165 g/5½oz dried spaghetti
2 tbsp olive oil, for cooking the balls
finely chopped basil leaves, to garnish

For the meatless balls

100 g/3½ oz TVP (textured vegetable
protein, available from most good health
food stores)
2 garlic cloves, peeled and crushed
3 tbsp soy sauce
2 tsp dried oregano
½ tsp ground cumin
250 ml/8 fl oz boiling water

For the tomato sauce

2 tbsp olive oil
1 onion, peeled and diced
3 garlic cloves, peeled and crushed
400 g/14 oz canned chopped tomatoes
¼ tsp salt
10 pitted green olives, sliced

Stir all the meatless balls ingredients together and leave for 15 minutes.

For the sauce, heat the oil in a pan over a medium heat and fry the onion for 5 minutes. Add the garlic and fry for 1 minute. Add the tomatoes, salt and olives. Bring to the boil, reduce the heat and simmer, uncovered, for 20 minutes.

Chop the TVP mixture in a food processor. Using your hands, form the mixture into small balls and set aside.

Cook the spaghetti in a pan of boiling water according to the packet instructions.

Heat the oil for cooking the balls in a frying pan over a medium heat and fry the balls for 3 minutes on each side until browned.

Stir the sauce through the spaghetti and top with the meatless balls and basil.

Cauliflower Mac 'n' Cheeze

Serves 4

1 small cauliflower, cut into florets
200 g/7 oz macaroni pasta
2 quantities Cheeze Sauce (*see* page 44)
crusty bread, to serve

Preheat the oven to 180°C/350°F/Gas Mark 4.

Steam the cauliflower for 15 minutes.

Cook the macaroni in a pan of boiling water according to the packet instructions.

Meanwhile, prepare the Cheeze Sauce according to page 44.

Once everything is ready, mix them together, then transfer to a baking dish and bake for 30–40 minutes until browned. Serve with bread or potatoes.

Beetroot Risotto

Serves 6

2 tbsp extra virgin olive oil
1 onion, peeled and finely chopped
2 garlic cloves, peeled and finely chopped
2 tsp freshly chopped thyme
1 tsp grated lemon rind
350 g/12 oz risotto rice
150 ml/1¼ pint dry vegan white wine
900 ml/1½ pints vegetable stock, heated
2 tbsp vegan cream alternative or coconut cream
225 g/8 oz cooked beetroot, peeled and finely chopped
2 tbsp freshly chopped parsley
75 g/3 oz Parmesan-style vegan cheese, freshly grated
salt and freshly ground black pepper
sprigs of fresh thyme, to garnish

Heat the oil in a large, heavy-based frying pan. Add the onion, garlic, thyme and lemon rind. Cook gently for 5 minutes, stirring frequently, until the onion is soft and transparent but not coloured. Add the rice and stir until it is well coated in the oil.

Add the wine, then bring to the boil and boil rapidly until the wine has almost evaporated. Reduce the heat.

Keeping the pan over a low heat, add a ladleful of the hot stock to the rice and cook, stirring constantly, until the stock is absorbed. Continue gradually adding the stock in this way until the rice is tender; this should take about 20 minutes. You may not need all the stock.

Stir in the cream, chopped beetroot, parsley and half the grated cheese. Season to taste with salt and pepper. Garnish with sprigs of fresh thyme and serve immediately with the remaining grated cheese.

Stir Fries
& Curries

Who needs meat when you have a world of flavours, seasonings and spices from which to choose when making stir fries and curries? Whether it's East Asia's ginger, rice vinegar and soy sauce, or Thailand's lemongrass and coconut milk, or the cardamom, cumin and turmeric of India, to name but a few, you will be able to create zingy and lip-smacking dishes easily. Why not try the comforting Pad Thai Noodles with Mushrooms or the warming Mung Bean Curry?

Thai Stir Fry with Tofu

Serves 4

450 g/1 lb tofu
2 tbsp dry sherry
125 g/4 oz medium rice noodles
125 g/4 oz mangetout, halved
3 tbsp groundnut oil
1 onion, peeled and finely sliced
1 garlic clove, peeled and finely sliced
2.5 cm/1 inch piece fresh root ginger,
peeled and finely sliced
125 g/4 oz beansprouts
2 tbsp light soy sauce
½ tsp sugar
salt and freshly ground black pepper
½ courgette, cut into matchsticks

To garnish

2 tbsp roasted peanuts, roughly chopped
sprigs of fresh basil

Cut the tofu into cubes and place in a bowl. Sprinkle over the sherry and toss to coat. Cover loosely and leave to marinate in the refrigerator for 30 minutes.

Bring a large saucepan of lightly salted water to the boil and add the noodles and mangetout. Simmer for 3 minutes or according to the packet instructions, then drain and rinse under cold running water. Leave to drain again.

Heat a wok or large frying pan, add the oil and when hot, add the onion and stir-fry for 2–3 minutes. Add the garlic and ginger and stir-fry for 30 seconds. Add the beansprouts and tofu, stir in the soy sauce with the sugar and season to taste with salt and pepper.

Stir-fry the tofu mixture over a medium heat for 2–3 minutes, then add the courgettes, noodles and mangetout and stir-fry for a further 1–2 minutes. Tip into a warmed serving dish or spoon on to individual plates. Sprinkle with the peanuts, add a sprig of basil and serve immediately.

Fried Rice with Bamboo Shoots & Ginger

Serves 4

4 tbsp sunflower oil

1 onion, peeled and finely chopped

225 g/8 oz long-grain rice

3 garlic cloves, peeled and cut into slivers

2.5 cm/1 inch piece fresh root ginger, peeled and grated

3 spring onions, trimmed and chopped

450 ml/¾ pint vegetable stock

125 g/4 oz button mushrooms, wiped and halved

75 g/3 oz frozen peas, thawed

2 tbsp light soy sauce

500 g can bamboo shoots, drained and thinly sliced

salt and freshly ground black pepper

cayenne pepper, to taste

fresh coriander leaves, to garnish

Heat a wok, add the oil and when hot, add the onion and cook gently for 3–4 minutes, then add the long-grain rice and cook for 3–4 minutes or until golden, stirring frequently.

Add the garlic, ginger and chopped spring onions to the wok and stir well. Pour the stock into a small saucepan and bring to the boil. Carefully ladle the hot stock into the wok, stir well, then simmer gently for 10 minutes or until most of the liquid has been absorbed.

Stir the button mushrooms, peas and soy sauce into the wok and continue to cook for a further 5 minutes, or until the rice is tender, adding a little extra stock if necessary.

Add the bamboo shoots to the wok and carefully stir in. Season to taste with salt, pepper and cayenne pepper. Cook for 2–3 minutes or until heated through. Tip on to a warmed serving dish, garnish with coriander leaves and serve immediately.

Singapore Noodles

Serves 4

225 g/8 oz thin round rice noodles
3 tbsp groundnut or vegetable oil
125 g/4 oz field mushrooms, wiped and thinly sliced
2.5 cm/1 inch piece root ginger, peeled and finely chopped
1 red chilli, deseeded and thinly sliced
1 red pepper, deseeded and thinly sliced
2 garlic cloves, peeled and crushed
1 medium courgette, cut in half lengthwise and diagonally sliced
4–6 spring onions, trimmed and thinly sliced
50 g/2 oz frozen garden peas, thawed
1 tbsp curry paste
2 tbsp tomato ketchup
salt or soy sauce
125 g/4 oz beansprouts, rinsed and drained

To garnish
sesame seeds
fresh coriander leaves

Bring a large pan of lightly salted water to a rolling boil. Add the noodles and cook according to the packet instructions, or until *al dente*. Drain thoroughly and toss with 1 tablespoon of the oil.

Heat the remaining oil in a wok or large frying pan over high heat. Add the mushrooms, ginger, chilli and red pepper and stir-fry for 2 minutes. Add the garlic, courgettes, spring onions and garden peas and stir lightly.

Push the vegetables to one side and add the curry paste, tomato ketchup and about 125 ml/4 fl oz hot water. Season to taste with salt or a few drops of soy sauce and allow to boil vigorously, stirring, until the paste is smooth.

Stir the reserved noodles and the beansprouts into the vegetable mixture and stir-fry until coated with the paste and thoroughly heated through. Season with more soy sauce if necessary, then turn into a large warmed serving bowl or spoon on to individual plates. Garnish with sesame seeds and coriander leaves. Serve immediately.

Mixed Vegetables Stir Fry

Serves 4

2 tbsp groundnut oil

4 garlic cloves, peeled and finely sliced

2.5 cm/1 inch piece fresh root ginger, peeled and finely sliced

75 g/3 oz broccoli florets

50 g/2 oz mangetout, trimmed

75 g/3 oz carrots, peeled and cut into matchsticks

1 green pepper, deseeded and cut into strips

1 red pepper, deseeded and cut into strips

1 tbsp soy sauce

1 tbsp hoisin sauce

1 tsp sugar

salt and freshly ground black pepper

4 spring onions, trimmed and shredded, to garnish

Heat a wok, add the oil and when hot, add the garlic and ginger slices and stir-fry for 1 minute.

Add the broccoli florets to the wok, stir-fry for 1 minute, then add the mangetout, carrots and the green and red peppers and stir-fry for a further 3–4 minutes, or until tender but still crisp.

Blend the soy sauce, hoisin sauce and sugar in a small bowl. Stir well, season to taste with salt and pepper and pour into the wok. Transfer the vegetables to a warmed serving dish. Garnish with shredded spring onions and serve immediately with a selection of other Thai dishes.

Spicy Cucumber Stir Fry

Serves 4

25 g/1 oz black soya beans, soaked in
cold water, overnight
1½ cucumbers
2 tsp salt
1 tbsp groundnut oil
½ tsp mild chilli powder
4 garlic cloves, peeled and crushed
5 tbsp vegetable stock
1 tsp sesame oil
1 tbsp freshly chopped parsley, to garnish

Rinse the soaked beans thoroughly, then drain. Place in a saucepan, cover with cold water and bring to the boil, skimming off any scum that rises to the surface. Boil for 10 minutes, then reduce the heat and simmer for 1–1½ hours. Drain and reserve.

Peel the cucumbers, slice lengthways and remove the seeds. Cut into 2.5 cm/1 inch slices and place in a colander over a bowl. Sprinkle the salt over the cucumber and leave for 30 minutes. Rinse thoroughly in cold water, drain and pat dry with absorbent kitchen paper.

Heat a wok or large frying pan, add the oil and when hot, add the chilli powder, garlic and black beans and stir-fry for 30 seconds. Add the cucumber and stir-fry for 20 seconds.

Pour the stock into the wok and cook for 3–4 minutes, or until the cucumber is very tender. The liquid will have evaporated at this stage. Remove from the heat and stir in the sesame oil. Turn into a warmed serving dish, garnish with chopped parsley and serve immediately.

Chinese Leaves with Sweet & Sour Sauce

Serves 4

1 head Chinese leaves
200 g pack pak choi
1 tbsp cornflour
1 tbsp soy sauce
2 tbsp brown sugar
3 tbsp red wine vinegar
3 tbsp orange juice
2 tbsp tomato purée
3 tbsp sunflower oil
15 g/½ oz non-dairy margarine
1 tsp salt
2 tbsp toasted sesame seeds

Discard any tough outer leaves and stalks from the Chinese leaves and pak choi and wash well. Drain thoroughly and pat dry with absorbent kitchen paper. Shred the Chinese leaves and pak choi lengthways. Reserve.

In a small bowl, blend the cornflour with 4 tablespoons of water. Add the soy sauce, sugar, vinegar, orange juice and tomato purée and stir until blended thoroughly.

Pour the sauce into a small saucepan and bring to the boil. Simmer gently for 2–3 minutes, or until the sauce is thickened and smooth.

Meanwhile, heat a wok or large frying pan and add the sunflower oil and margarine. When melted, add the prepared Chinese leaves and pak choi, sprinkle with the salt and stir-fry for 2 minutes. Reduce the heat and cook gently for a further 1–2 minutes or until tender.

Transfer the Chinese leaves and pak choi to a warmed serving platter and drizzle over the warm sauce. Sprinkle with the toasted sesame seeds and serve immediately.

Pad Thai Noodles
with Mushrooms

Serves 4

125 g/4 oz flat rice noodles or rice vermicelli
1 tbsp vegetable oil
2 garlic cloves, peeled and finely chopped
225 g/8 oz mixed mushrooms, including
shiitake, oyster, field, brown and
wild mushrooms
2 tbsp lemon juice or 4 lemongrass stalks,
outer leaves discarded and finely chopped
1½ tbsp light soy sauce (optional)
½ tsp sugar
½ tsp cayenne pepper
2 spring onions, trimmed and cut into
2.5 cm/1 inch pieces
50 g/2 oz fresh beansprouts

To garnish
chopped roasted peanuts
freshly chopped coriander

Cook the noodles according to the packet instructions. Drain well and reserve.

Heat a wok or large frying pan. Add the oil and garlic. Fry until just golden.

Cook for a few seconds before adding the noodles and mushrooms. Scrape down the sides of the pan to ensure they mix with the garlic.

Add the lemon juice or lemongrass, soy sauce (if using), sugar, cayenne pepper, spring onions and half of the beansprouts, stirring quickly all the time.

Cook over a high heat for a further 2–3 minutes until everything is heated through.

Turn on to a serving plate. Top with the remaining beansprouts. Garnish with the chopped peanuts and coriander and serve immediately.

Fragrant Vegetable Pot

Serves 4

1 tbsp groundnut or vegetable oil
1 cinnamon stick, bruised
3 star anise
small piece fresh root ginger, peeled and grated
1 bird's eye red chilli, deseeded and chopped
300 g/10 oz Thai fragrant rice
1.2 litres/2¼ pints vegetable stock
225 g/8 oz broccoli, divided into tiny florets
225 g/8 oz French beans, trimmed and halved
1 red pepper, deseeded and chopped
1 orange pepper, deseeded and chopped
100 g/4 oz sugar snap peas, trimmed
100 g/4 oz baby corn
1 tbsp freshly chopped coriander, to garnish (optional)

Heat the oil in a large wok or heavy-based saucepan and add the spices, including the chilli. Cook for 2 minutes, stirring constantly.

Add the rice and stir until lightly coated in the spices and oil. Pour in half the stock, bring to the boil and cook for 10 minutes.

Add the remaining stock, the broccoli, French beans and chopped peppers and cook for a further 10 minutes. Add the sugar snap peas and baby corn and cook for 5–8 minutes, or until the vegetables are tender. Remove and discard the cinnamon stick and star anise and serve sprinkled with chopped coriander, if using.

Spiced Tomato Pilau

Serves 2-3

225 g/8 oz basmati rice
40 g/1½ oz non-dairy margarine
4 green cardamom pods
2 star anise
4 whole cloves
10 black peppercorns
5 cm/2 inch piece cinnamon stick
1 large red onion, peeled and finely sliced
175 g/6 oz canned chopped tomatoes
salt and freshly ground black pepper
sprigs of fresh coriander, to garnish

Wash the rice in several changes of water until the water remains relatively clear. Drain the rice and cover with fresh water. Leave to soak for 30 minutes. Drain well and reserve.

Heat a wok or large frying pan, then melt the margarine and add the cardamoms, star anise, cloves, black peppercorns and the cinnamon stick. Cook gently for 30 seconds. Increase the heat and add the onion. Cook for 7–8 minutes, until tender and starting to brown. Add the drained rice and cook for a further 2–3 minutes.

Sieve the tomatoes and mix with sufficient warm water to make 450 ml/16 fl oz. Pour this into the wok or frying pan, season to taste with salt and pepper and bring to the boil.

Cover, reduce the heat to very low and cook for 10 minutes. Remove from the heat and leave covered for a further 10 minutes. Do not lift the lid during cooking or resting. Finally, uncover and mix well with a fork, then heat for 1 minute. Garnish with the sprigs of fresh coriander and serve immediately.

Thai-style Cauliflower & Potato Curry

Serves 4

450 g/1 lb new potatoes, peeled and halved or quartered

350 g/12 oz cauliflower florets

3 garlic cloves, peeled and crushed

1 onion, peeled and finely chopped

40 g/1½ oz ground almonds

1 tsp ground coriander

½ tsp ground cumin

½ tsp turmeric

3 tbsp groundnut oil

salt and freshly ground black pepper

50 g/2 oz creamed coconut, broken into small pieces

200 ml/7 fl oz vegetable stock

1 tbsp mango chutney

sprigs of fresh coriander, to garnish

freshly cooked long-grain rice, to serve

Bring a saucepan of lightly salted water to the boil, add the potatoes and cook for 15 minutes or until just tender. Drain and leave to cool. Boil the cauliflower for 2 minutes, then drain and refresh under cold running water. Drain again and reserve.

Meanwhile, blend the garlic, onion, ground almonds and spices with 2 tablespoons of the oil, and salt and pepper to taste in a food processor until a smooth paste is formed. Heat a wok, add the remaining oil and, when hot, add the spice paste and cook for 3–4 minutes, stirring continuously.

Dissolve the creamed coconut in 6 tablespoons of boiling water and add to the wok. Pour in the stock, cook for 2–3 minutes, then stir in the cooked potatoes and cauliflower.

Stir in the mango chutney and heat through for 3–4 minutes or until piping hot. Tip into a warmed serving dish, garnish with sprigs of fresh coriander and serve immediately with freshly cooked rice.

Thai Green Curry

Serves 4

150 g/5 oz/generous black rice
1 bay leaf
200 g/7 oz chestnut (cremini) mushrooms,
quartered
400 ml/14 fl oz canned coconut milk
200 ml/7 fl oz vegan stock (be aware that
many vegetarian stock cubes contain whey)
2 tbsp soy sauce
200 g/7 oz green beans, trimmed
400 g/14 oz tofu, cubed
75 g/3 oz frozen petit pois
1 handful Thai basil leaves

For the paste
6 kaffir lime leaves
1 mild green chili, deseeded
2 lemongrass stalks, tough layers removed
2.5 cm/1 inch ginger root
2 garlic cloves
2 handfuls coriander
4 spring onions
50 ml/2 fl oz melted coconut oil

Cook the black rice according to the packet instructions. For the paste, blitz all the ingredients in a small food processor or use a handheld blender.

Fry the paste in a pan over a medium-low heat for 1 minute. Add the bay leaf and mushrooms and cook for 5 minutes.

Add the milk, stock, soy sauce and beans and bring to the boil. Add the tofu and petit pois and return to the boil.

Reduce the heat and simmer for 5–7 minutes. Stir through the basil and serve.

Coconut Dhal & Pilau Rice

Serves 2

For the coconut dhal

1 tbsp coconut oil
1 tsp mustard seeds
½ tsp cumin seeds
1 tsp ground turmeric
1 tsp ground coriander
1 small onion, peeled and diced
1 large dried red chili
1 tomato, chopped
100 g/3½ oz dried red lentils
200 ml/7 fl oz coconut milk
125 ml/4 fl oz water
large pinch salt

For the pilau rice

2 tbsp vegetable oil
1 small onion, peeled and finely sliced
1 tsp cumin seeds
6 cardamom pods
1 cinnamon stick; 3 cloves
150 g/5 oz basmati rice
300 ml/10 fl oz water

For the topping

1 tbsp coriander leaves
hot red chili sauce (optional)

For the dhal, heat the coconut oil and mustard seeds in a pan with the lid on. When the mustard seeds start to pop, add the spices and onion and cook over a medium heat for 5–10 minutes. Add the remaining ingredients. Bring to the boil, stirring frequently. Reduce the heat and simmer for 35 minutes, stirring occasionally.

For the rice, heat the vegetable oil until it is very hot and fry the onion until brown and crispy. Remove the onion and set aside. Add the spices and fry over a medium heat for 1 minute. Add the rice and fry for 2 minutes, stirring. Add the water, bring to the boil, reduce the heat, cover and simmer for 10 minutes until the rice is cooked.

Serve the dhal on a bed of rice, topped with coriander and red chili sauce, if liked.

Vegetable Biryani

Serves 4

2 tbsp vegetable oil, plus a little extra
for brushing
2 large onions, peeled and thinly
sliced lengthways
2 garlic cloves, peeled and finely chopped
2.5 cm/1 inch piece fresh root ginger,
peeled and finely grated
1 small carrot, peeled and cut into sticks
1 small parsnip, peeled and diced
1 small sweet potato, peeled and diced
1 tbsp medium curry paste
225 g/8 oz basmati rice
4 ripe tomatoes, peeled, deseeded
and diced
600 ml/1 pint vegetable stock
175 g/6 oz cauliflower florets
50 g/2 oz peas, thawed if frozen
salt and freshly ground black pepper

To garnish

Crispy onion rings; freshly ground black
pepper; roasted cashew nuts; raisins and
fresh coriander leaves.

Preheat the oven to 200°C/400°F/Gas Mark 6. Put 1 tablespoon of the vegetable oil in a large bowl with the onions and toss to coat. Lightly brush or spray a nonstick baking sheet with a little more oil. Spread half the onions on the baking sheet and cook at the top of the preheated oven for 15–20 minutes, stirring regularly, until golden and crisp. Remove from the oven and reserve for the garnish.

Meanwhile, heat a large ovenproof casserole over a medium heat and add the remaining oil and onions. Cook for 5–7 minutes until softened and starting to brown. Add a little water if they start to stick. Add the garlic and ginger and cook for another minute, then add the carrot, parsnip and sweet potato. Cook the vegetables for a further 5 minutes. Add the curry paste and stir for a minute until everything is coated, then stir in the rice and tomatoes. After 2 minutes, add the stock and stir well. Bring to the boil, cover and simmer over a very gentle heat for about 10 minutes.

Add the cauliflower and peas and cook for 8–10 minutes, or until the rice is tender. Season to taste with salt and pepper. Serve garnished with the crispy onions, cashew nuts, raisins and coriander. To alleviate the dryness, biryani is best served with dhal and raita.

Creamy Chickpea Curry

Serves 4–6

2 tbsp vegetable oil
1 cinnamon stick, bruised
3 cardamom pods, bruised
1 tsp fennel seeds
5 cm/2 inch piece fresh root ginger, peeled and grated
2 garlic cloves, peeled and crushed
2 red chillies, deseeded and chopped
1 large onion, peeled and chopped
1 tsp ground fenugreek
1 tsp garam masala
½ tsp turmeric
2 x 400 g/14 oz cans chickpeas, drained and rinsed
300 ml/½ pint water
1 tsp tomato purée
300 ml/½ pint coconut milk
225 g/8 oz cherry tomatoes, halved
2 tbsp freshly chopped coriander

Heat the oil in a frying pan, add the cinnamon stick, cardamom pods, fennel seeds and ginger and cook gently for 3 minutes, stirring frequently. Add the garlic, chillies, onion and remaining spices to the pan and cook gently, stirring occasionally, for 3–5 minutes, or until the onion has softened.

Add the chickpeas and water. Bring to the boil, then reduce the heat and simmer for 15 minutes.

Blend the tomato purée with a little of the coconut milk then add to the chickpeas with the remaining coconut milk and tomatoes. Cook for 8–10 minutes, or until the tomatoes have begun to collapse. Stir in the chopped coriander and serve.

Mung Bean Curry

Serves 4–6

50 g/2 oz creamed coconut
2 red chillies, deseeded and finely chopped
250 ml/8 fl oz water
250 g/9 oz canned mung beans
½ tsp turmeric
225 g/8 oz potatoes, peeled
1 onion, peeled and cut into wedges
175 g/6 oz French beans, trimmed
and chopped
2 tbsp vegetable oil
1 tsp brown mustard seeds
5–6 curry leaves

Break the coconut into small pieces and place in a food processor or liquidiser with 1 of the chillies and 3 tablespoons water. Blend for 1 minute, then, with the motor still running, gradually pour in the remaining water to form a thin smooth liquid. Reserve.

Place the mung beans, remaining chilli and turmeric in a saucepan and cover with water. Bring to the boil, then reduce the heat and simmer for 20 minutes. Cut the potatoes into small chunks and add to the saucepan, together with the onion and French beans. Continue to cook for 8 minutes.

Pour in the coconut liquid and cook, stirring occasionally, for a further 10 minutes, or until the beans and vegetables are tender.

Meanwhile, heat the oil in a small frying pan, add the mustard seeds and the curry leaves and fry for 1 minute, or until the mustard seeds pop. Stir well, then stir into the curry. Serve.

Sweet Potato Curry

Serves 4–6

2 tbsp vegetable oil

2 green chillies, deseeded and chopped

5 cm/2 inch piece fresh root ginger, peeled and grated

½–1 tsp chilli powder

1 tsp turmeric

1 tsp ground cumin

1 tsp ground coriander

2 onions, peeled and cut into wedges

2–3 garlic cloves, peeled and crushed

450 g/1 lb sweet potatoes, peeled and cut into small chunks

1 large green pepper, deseeded and chopped

4 tomatoes, chopped

300 ml/½ pint coconut milk

225 g/8 oz fresh spinach leaves

few curry leaves

Heat the oil in a sauté pan or wok, add the chillies, ginger and spices and fry for 3 minutes, stirring frequently. Add the onions and garlic and continue to fry for a further 5 minutes, or until the onion has softened.

Add the sweet potatoes and stir until coated in the spices, then add the green pepper and chopped tomatoes.

Pour in the coconut milk. Bring to the boil, then reduce the heat, cover and simmer for 12–15 minutes, or until the vegetables are cooked. Stir in the spinach and heat for 3 minutes, or until wilted. Add the curry leaves, stir and serve.

Calypso Rice with Curried Bananas

℃

Serves 4

2 tbsp vegetable oil
1 onion, peeled and finely chopped
1 garlic clove, peeled and crushed
1 red chilli, deseeded and finely chopped
1 red pepper, deseeded and chopped
225 g/8 oz basmati rice
juice of 1 lime
350 ml/12 fl oz vegetable stock
200 g can black-eye beans, drained
and rinsed
2 tbsp freshly chopped parsley
salt and freshly ground black pepper
sprigs of coriander, to garnish

For the curried bananas

4 green bananas
2 tbsp vegetable oil
200 ml/7 fl oz coconut milk
2 tsp mild curry paste

Heat the oil in a large frying pan and gently cook the onion for 10 minutes until soft. Add the garlic, chilli and red pepper and cook for 2–3 minutes. Rinse the rice under cold running water, then add to the pan and stir. Pour in the lime juice and stock, bring to the boil, cover and simmer for 12–15 minutes, or until the rice is tender and the stock is absorbed.

Stir in the black-eye beans and chopped parsley and season to taste with salt and pepper. Leave to stand, covered, for 5 minutes before serving, to allow the beans to warm through.

While the rice is cooking, make the Curried Bananas. Remove the skins from the bananas – they may need to be cut off with a sharp knife. Slice the flesh thickly. Heat the oil in a frying pan and cook the bananas, in 2 batches, for 2–3 minutes, or until lightly browned.

Pour the coconut milk into the pan and stir in the curry paste. Add the banana slices to the coconut milk and simmer, uncovered, over a low heat for 8–10 minutes, or until the bananas are very soft and the coconut milk slightly reduced.

Spoon the rice onto warmed serving plates, garnish with coriander and serve immediately with the Curried Bananas.

Treats & Desserts

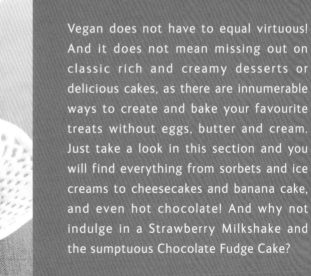

Vegan does not have to equal virtuous! And it does not mean missing out on classic rich and creamy desserts or delicious cakes, as there are innumerable ways to create and bake your favourite treats without eggs, butter and cream. Just take a look in this section and you will find everything from sorbets and ice creams to cheesecakes and banana cake, and even hot chocolate! And why not indulge in a Strawberry Milkshake and the sumptuous Chocolate Fudge Cake?

Coconut Sorbet with Mango Sauce

Serves 4

½ teaspoon powdered agar-agar
250 g/9 oz caster sugar
600 ml/1 pint coconut milk
2 mangos, peeled, pitted and sliced
2 tbsp icing sugar
zest and juice of 1 lime

Set the freezer to rapid freeze, 2 hours before freezing the sorbet.

Meanwhile, place agar-agar, caster sugar and 300 ml/½ pint of the coconut milk in a heavy-based saucepan and bring to the boil over medium heat, stirring until the agar-agar and sugar has dissolved. Remove from the heat.

Stir in the remaining coconut milk. Leave until cold.

Pour the agar-agar and coconut mixture into a freezable container and place in the freezer. Leave for at least 1 hour, or until the mixture has started to form ice crystals. Remove and beat with a spoon, then return to the freezer and continue to freeze until the mixture is frozen, beating at least twice more during this time.

Meanwhile, make the sauce. Place the sliced mango, icing sugar and the lime zest and juice in a food processor and blend until smooth. Spoon into a small jug.

Leave the sorbet to soften in the refrigerator for at least 30 minutes before serving. Serve scoops of sorbet on individual plates with a little of the mango sauce poured over. Remember to turn the freezer to normal setting.

Raspberry Sorbet Crush

Serves 4

225 g/8 oz raspberries, thawed if frozen

grated rind and juice of 1 lime

300 ml/½ pint orange juice

225 g/8 oz caster sugar

2 'egg white'-portions egg-replacer (*see* page 29), or 4 tbsp aquafaba (chickpea water)

Set the freezer to rapid freeze. If using fresh raspberries pick over and lightly rinse. Place the raspberries in a dish and, using a masher, mash to a chunky purée.

Place the lime rind and juice, orange juice and half the caster sugar in a large heavy-based saucepan. Heat gently stirring frequently until the sugar is dissolved. Bring to the boil and boil rapidly for about 5 minutes.

Remove the pan from the heat and pour carefully into a freezable container. Leave to cool, then place in the freezer and freeze for 2 hours, stirring occasionally to break up the ice crystals.

Fold the ice mixture into the raspberry purée with a metal spoon and freeze for a further 2 hours, stirring occasionally.

Whisk the egg-replacer or aquafaba until stiff. Then gradually whisk in the remaining caster sugar a tablespoon at a time until the mixture is stiff and glossy.

Fold into the raspberry sorbet with a metal spoon and freeze for 1 hour. Spoon into tall glasses and serve immediately. Remember to return the freezer to its normal setting.

Vegan Ice Cream

Serves 2

4 frozen bananas
2 tsp vanilla extract
3 tbsp water

(Prepare frozen bananas by peeling ripe bananas and cutting into large slices before freezing.)

Using a blender, blitz all the ingredients until smooth. Eat immediately or freeze for later. If you freeze it, remove from the freezer 10 minutes before serving to soften. Store in the freezer for up to a month.

Variations: Create different flavours by trying different combinations of frozen fruit and/or flavouring when blending.

Strawberry Milkshake

Makes 1 large
or 2 smaller glasses

300 g/11 oz frozen strawberries
125 ml/4 fl oz frozen full-fat canned
coconut milk (freeze in an ice tray
in advance)
1–2 tbsp maple syrup or other vegan
sweetener
½ tsp balsamic vinegar (optional)
few fresh strawberries, for topping

Blend all the ingredients until thoroughly combined. Balsamic vinegar may seem like a strange ingredient to add to strawberry milkshake, but it creates a special alchemy that brings out the flavour of the strawberries.

Spoon into tall glasses and top with fresh strawberries and serve.

Strawberry Cheesecake Pots

Makes 4

For the base

2 Shortbreads (*see* page 238) or plain
vegan biscuits, broken into fine crumbs
pinch salt

For the filling

130 g/4½ oz cashew nuts
2 tsp lemon zest (about 1 lemon)
2 tbsp lemon juice
3 tbsp melted coconut oil
50 ml/2 fl oz water
1 tbsp vanilla extract
1 tsp maple syrup
½ tsp nutritional yeast flakes (optional)

For the topping

6 tbsp good strawberry jam
2 tbsp water
6 fresh strawberries, sliced
mint leaves, to decorate (optional)

For the base, divide the biscuit crumbs evenly among 4 small glasses or jars and firm down using the back of a teaspoon.

For the filling, blend all the ingredients until smooth and creamy. Spoon on top of the bases.

For the topping, mix the strawberry jam and water together. Pour a thin layer on top of each filling. Top with strawberries and pour the remaining jam over. Add a mint sprig, if liked, and chill for 1 hour.

Note: To prepare in advance, follow the recipe until the topping, then freeze. Remove from the freezer 4–8 hours before eating, adding the fruit topping.

Apple & Berry Crumble with Custard

Serves 4

For the dried apple

1 eating apple

For the filling

4 peeled and cored eating apples

350 g/12 oz frozen or fresh mixed berries

65 g/2½ oz unrefined granulated sugar

1 tsp vanilla extract

For the crumble

125 g/4 oz plain flour

50 g/2 oz caster sugar, plus extra for sprinkling

2 tbsp melted coconut oil

pinch salt

1 tsp ground cinnamon

custard (*see* page 42), to serve

Preheat the oven to 95°C/200°F/Gas Mark 1/4. For the dried apple, finely slice the apple across its body with a large sharp knife or mandoline. Place the slices on greaseproof (wax) paper on a rimmed baking sheet and bake for 2–3 hours. Turn the oven off and leave them to cool in the oven for another hour.

For the filling, preheat the oven to 190°C/375°F/Gas Mark 5. Cut the apples into bite-size chunks. Set aside a handful of berries for topping, then mix the remaining berries with the apple chunks, sugar and vanilla. Divide the fruit mix between 4 heatproof bowls.

To make the topping, mix the flour, sugar, oil, salt and cinnamon together in a bowl. Sprinkle over the filling. Scatter a few berries on top and sprinkle with a little more sugar.

Place the bowls on a rimmed baking sheet and cook in the oven for 35 minutes until golden. Top with dried apple. Serve hot, with custard (*see* page 42).

Orange Curd & Plum Pie

Serves 4

700 g/1½ lb plums, stoned and quartered
2 tbsp light brown sugar
grated zest of ½ lemon
25 g/1 oz dairy-free margarine, melted
1 tbsp olive oil
6 sheets filo pastry
½ x 411 g jar luxury orange curd
50 g/2 oz sultanas
icing sugar, to decorate
vegan yogurt, to serve (*see* page 40)

Preheat the oven to 200°C/400°F/Gas Mark 6. Lightly oil a 20.5 cm/8 inch round cake tin. Cook the plums with 2 tablespoons of the light brown sugar for 8–10 minutes to soften them, remove from the heat and reserve.

Mix together the lemon zest, margarine and oil. Lay a sheet of pastry in the prepared cake tin and brush with the lemon zest mixture.

Cut the sheets of filo pastry in half and then place one half in the cake tin and brush again.

Top with the remaining halved sheets of pastry, brushing each time with the lemon zest mixture. Fold each sheet in half lengthways to line the sides of the tin to make a filo case.

Mix together the plums, orange curd and sultanas and spoon into the pastry case.

Draw the pastry edges up over the filling to enclose. Brush the remaining sheets of filo pastry with the lemon zest mixture and cut into thick strips.

Scrunch each strip of pastry and arrange on top of the pie. Bake in the preheated oven for 25 minutes until golden. Sprinkle with icing sugar and serve with the yogurt.

Chocolate Hazelnut Crêpes

Makes 8 crêpes

2 tbsp ground flaxseed
350 ml/12 fl oz unsweetened dairy-free milk
75 g/3 oz plain flour
pinch salt
1½ tsp vegetable oil, plus extra for brushing

For the chocolate hazelnut spread (makes 250 ml/8 fl oz)

125 ml/4 fl oz coconut oil
6 tbsp unsweetened cocoa powder
6 tbsp maple syrup
50 g/2 oz ground toasted hazelnuts (grind in a spice grinder or high-speed blender)
1 tsp vanilla extract
pinch salt

For the spread, melt the coconut oil in a heatproof bowl set over just-boiled water. Stir in the remaining ingredients and mix until smooth. Spoon into a sterilized jar.

To make the crêpes, combine the ground flaxseed, milk, flour, salt and vegetable oil in a blender until smooth. Cover and chill for 1 hour.

Heat a frying pan over a medium-high heat and brush with vegetable oil. Pour 50 ml/2 fl oz of the batter into the pan, tilting to coat the surface of the pan and cook for 1–2 minutes until golden. Carefully flip and cook for another 1–2 minutes. Repeat with the remaining batter.

Spread 2 tablespoons of the chocolate hazelnut spread onto each crêpe, fold into quarters and serve in a pretty pile.

Banana Cake

Cuts into 8 slices

3 medium-sized ripe bananas
1 tsp lemon juice
150 g/5 oz soft brown sugar
75 g/3 oz non-dairy margarine
250 g/9 oz self-raising flour
1 tsp ground cinnamon
3 portions egg-replacer (*see* page 29)
50 g/2 oz walnuts, chopped
1 tsp each ground cinnamon and caster sugar, to decorate

Preheat the oven to 190°C/375°F/Gas Mark 5 10 minutes before baking. Lightly oil and line the base of an 18 cm/7 inch deep round cake tin with greaseproof or baking paper.

Mash 2 of the bananas in a small bowl, sprinkle with the lemon juice and a heaped tablespoon of the sugar. Mix together lightly and reserve.

Gently heat the remaining sugar and margarine in a small saucepan until the margarine has just melted.

Pour into a small bowl, then allow to cool slightly. Sift the flour and cinnamon into a large bowl and make a well in the centre.

Beat the egg-replacer into the cooled sugar mixture, pour into the well of flour, and mix thoroughly.

Gently stir in the mashed banana mixture. Pour half of the mixture into the prepared tin. Thinly slice the remaining banana and arrange over the cake mixture. Sprinkle over the chopped walnuts, then cover with the remaining cake mixture.

Bake in the preheated oven for 50–55 minutes, or until well risen and golden brown. Allow to cool in the tin, turn out and sprinkle with the ground cinnamon and caster sugar. Serve hot or cold with a jug of chilled vegan cream alternative for pouring.

Peanut Butter Truffle Cookies

Makes 18

125 g/4 oz dairy-free dark chocolate
150 ml/¼ pint coconut cream
125 g/4 oz non-dairy margarine, softened
125 g/4 oz caster sugar
125 g/4 oz crunchy or smooth peanut butter
4 tbsp golden syrup
1 tbsp unsweetened almond or soya milk
225 g/8 oz plain flour
½ tsp bicarbonate of soda

Preheat the oven to 180°C/350°F/Gas Mark 4 10 minutes before baking. Make the chocolate filling by breaking the chocolate into small pieces and placing in a heatproof bowl.

Put the coconut cream into a saucepan and heat to boiling point. Immediately pour over the chocolate. Leave to stand for 1–2 minutes, then stir until smooth. Set aside to cool until firm enough to scoop. Do not refrigerate.

Lightly oil a baking sheet. Cream together the margarine and the sugar until light and fluffy. Blend in the peanut butter, followed by the golden syrup and milk.

Sift together the flour and bicarbonate of soda. Add to the peanut butter mixture, mix well and knead until smooth.

Flatten 1–2 tablespoons of the cookie mixture on a chopping board.

Put a spoonful of the chocolate mixture into the centre of the cookie dough, then fold the dough around the chocolate to enclose completely.

Put the balls on to the baking sheet and flatten slightly. Bake in the preheated oven for 10–12 minutes until golden.

Remove from the oven and transfer to a wire rack to cool completely and serve.

Shortbread

Makes about 10 biscuits

200 g/7 oz plain flour, plus extra for dusting
50 g/2 oz caster sugar, plus extra for sprinkling
generous pinch salt
100 g/3½ oz coconut oil

Preheat the oven to 170°C/325°F/Gas Mark 3 and line a rimmed baking sheet with greaseproof (wax) paper.

Mix the flour, sugar and salt together in a bowl. Rub in the oil with your fingertips until the mixture resembles soft breadcrumbs. Press together and flatten the dough out on greaseproof paper to 1 cm/½ inch thick, then cut out shapes with a cookie cutter. Using a spatula, gently move each biscuit to the baking sheet. Repeat until all the dough is used up.

Sprinkle with sugar, then bake for 20–30 minutes until pale golden. Leave on the baking sheet to cool completely before storing in an airtight container for up to 2 weeks in the refrigerator.

Oatmeal Coconut Cookies

Makes 40

225 g/8 oz non-dairy margarine
125 g/4 oz soft light brown sugar
125 g/4 oz caster sugar
1½ portions egg-replacer, lightly
beaten (*see* page 29)
1 tsp vanilla essence
225 g/8 oz plain flour
1 tsp baking powder
½ tsp bicarbonate of soda
125 g/4 oz rolled oats
75 g/3 oz desiccated coconut

Preheat the oven to 180°C/350°F/Gas Mark 4, 10 minutes before baking. Lightly oil a baking sheet.

Cream together the margarine and sugars until light and fluffy. Gradually stir in the egg-replacer and vanilla essence and beat until well blended.

Sift together the flour, baking powder and bicarbonate of soda in another bowl.

Add to the margarine and sugar mixture and beat together until smooth. Fold in the rolled oats and coconut with a metal spoon or rubber spatula.

Roll heaped teaspoonfuls of the mixture into balls and place on the baking sheet about 5 cm/2 inches apart and flatten each ball slightly with the heel of the hand. Transfer to the preheated oven and bake for 12–15 minutes, until just golden.

Remove from the oven and transfer the biscuits to a wire rack to completely cool and serve.

Lime Cheesecake

Makes enough for 12 slices

For the base
95 g/3 oz freshly ground raw almonds
¼ tsp mineral salt
85 g/3 oz Medjool dates, pitted and finely chopped

For the centre
225 g/8 oz cashew nuts
grated zest of 2 limes
50 ml/2 fl oz lime juice
50 ml/2 fl oz melted extra virgin coconut oil
100 ml/3½ fl oz water
2 tbsp vanilla extract
½ tsp nutritional yeast flakes

For the topping
75 g/3 oz cashew nuts
zest of 2 limes, plus extra to decorate
50 ml/2 fl oz lime juice
1 tbsp melted extra virgin coconut oil
¼ tsp spirulina powder

Sprinkle a small handful of the ground almonds onto the base of an 18 cm/7 inch loose-bottomed cake tin.

Place the remaining almonds into a bowl, add the salt and dates and knead together to form a dough. Using wet hands, press the dough into the base of the cake tin. Set aside.

Blend the ingredients for the centre together in a blender until smooth, then pour onto the cheesecake base.

Optional: to create the decorative green indentation in the cheesecake, push the edge of the spatula down at an angle about 2.5 cm/1 inch from the edge of the cake tin, and draw a 'ditch' around the cake at this angle.

Blend the topping ingredients together, then spread on top of the filling with a spatula, filling the ditch with topping.

Leave to set in the refrigerator for 2–4 hours.

Release the base of the cake tin and slide the cheesecake onto a plate. Decorate with lime zest.

Nutty Date Pudding with Chocolate Sauce

Serves 6-8

125 g/4 oz non-dairy margarine
125 g/4 oz golden caster sugar
3 portions egg-replacer, beaten (*see* page 29)
175 g/6 oz self-raising flour, sifted
50 g/2 oz dairy-free dark chocolate, grated
3 tbsp unsweetened almond or soya milk
75 g/3 oz hazelnuts, roughly chopped
75 g/3 oz stoned dates, roughly chopped
chopped toasted hazelnuts, to serve

For the chocolate sauce
50 g/2 oz margarine
50 g/2 oz soft light brown sugar
50 g/2 oz dairy-free dark chocolate, broken into pieces
125 ml/4 fl oz coconut cream

Lightly oil a 1.1 litre/2 pint pudding basin and line the base with a small circle of nonstick baking parchment. Cream the margarine and sugar together in a large bowl until light and fluffy. Add the beaten egg-replacer a little at a time, adding 1 tablespoon of the flour after each addition. When all of it has been added, stir in the remaining flour.

Add the grated chocolate and mix in lightly, then stir in the milk together with the hazelnuts and dates. Stir lightly until mixed together well.

Spoon the mixture into the prepared pudding basin and level the surface. Cover with a double sheet of baking parchment with a pleat in the centre, allowing for expansion, then cover either with a pudding cloth or a double sheet of tinfoil, again with a central pleat. Secure with string.

Place in the top of a steamer, set over a saucepan of gently simmering water and steam for 2 hours, or until cooked and firm to the touch. Remember to top up the water if necessary. Remove the pudding from the saucepan and leave to rest for 5 minutes, before turning out onto a serving plate. Discard the small circle of baking parchment, then sprinkle with the chopped toasted hazelnuts. Keep warm.

Meanwhile, make the sauce. Place the margarine, sugar and chocolate in a saucepan and heat until the chocolate has melted. Stir in the cream and simmer for 3 minutes until thickened. Pour over the pudding and serve.

Chocolate, Orange & Pine Nut Tart

Cuts into 8-10 slices

For the sweet shortcrust pastry

150 g/5 oz plain flour
½ tsp salt
3–4 tbsp icing sugar
125 g/4 oz non-dairy margarine, diced
2 portions egg-replacer, beaten (*see* page 29)
½ tsp vanilla essence

For the filling

125 g/4 oz dairy-free dark chocolate, chopped
60 g/2½ oz pine nuts, lightly toasted
3 portions egg-replacer
grated zest of 1 orange
1 tbsp Cointreau
225 ml/8 fl oz vegan cream
2 tbsp orange marmalade

Preheat the oven to 200°C/400°F/Gas Mark 6, 15 minutes before baking. Place the flour, salt and sugar in a food processor with the margarine and blend briefly. Add the egg-replacer, 2 tablespoons of iced water and the vanilla essence and blend until a soft dough is formed. Remove and knead until smooth, wrap in clingfilm and chill in the refrigerator for 1 hour.

Lightly oil a 23 cm/9 inch loose-based flan tin. Roll the dough out on a lightly floured surface to a 28 cm/11 inch round and use to line the tin. Press into the sides of the flan tin, crimp the edges, prick the base with a fork and chill in the refrigerator for 1 hour. Bake blind in the preheated oven for 10 minutes. Remove and place on a baking sheet. Reduce the oven temperature to 190°C/375°F/Gas Mark 5.

To make the filling, sprinkle the chocolate and the pine nuts evenly over the base of the pastry case. Beat the egg-replacer, orange zest, Cointreau and cream in a bowl until well blended, then pour over the chocolate and pine nuts.

Bake in the oven for 30 minutes, or until the pastry is golden and the custard mixture is just set. Transfer to a wire rack to cool slightly. Heat the marmalade with 1 tablespoon of water and brush over the tart. Serve warm or at room temperature.

Chocolate Fudge Cake

Makes 12 slices

For the cake

500 ml/18 fl oz unsweetened almond or soya milk

150 ml/5 fl oz melted coconut oil or light vegetable oil

2 tsp vanilla extract

325 g/11½ oz plain flour

400 g/14 oz unrefined granulated sugar

75 g/3 oz unsweetened cocoa powder

1 tsp salt

1 tsp cider vinegar

2 tsp bicarbonate of soda

For the frosting

125 ml/4 fl oz melted coconut oil

125 ml/4 fl oz water

1 tbsp vanilla extract

300 g/11 oz avocado, cubed

50 g/2 oz unsweetened cocoa powder

100 g/3½ oz icing sugar

2 pinches salt

Preheat the oven to 180°C/350°F/Gas Mark 4. Line two 20-cm/8-inch cake tins with greaseproof (wax) paper.

Blend all the cake ingredients, except the vinegar and bicarbonate of soda until smooth. Add the vinegar and bicarbonate of soda and blend for just long enough to mix into the batter. Do not over-blend or your cake will not rise well.

Divide the batter between the tins and bake for 30–40 minutes. After 30 minutes, test the cake by inserting a sharp knife or skewer – if it comes out with cake batter on it, cook for another 10 minutes.

Leave the cakes to stand for 10 minutes, then remove from their tins and cool on a wire rack. Cut the domed top off one of the cakes to make it flat.

Blend all the frosting ingredients together until smooth and creamy. Using a spatula, spread a generous layer of frosting on top of the flattened cake. Place the second cake on top and spread the remaining frosting over the cake.

Best eaten on the day of making, but will keep in a sealed container in the refrigerator for up to 3 days.

Cinnamon Hot Chocolate

Makes 1 mug

150 ml/¼ pint canned full-fat coconut milk
150 ml/¼ pint water
1 tsp ground cinnamon
½ tsp vanilla extract
pinch salt
1 tbsp unsweetened cocoa powder
1 tbsp maple syrup or
other vegan sweetener

Gently heat the milk, water, cinnamon, vanilla and salt in a small pan until just before boiling. Mix the cocoa and sweetener in a mug with 1 tablespoon of the hot milk mixture. Stir until smooth, then add the remaining milk.

Lemon Poppy Seed Cake

Makes 12 slices

125 ml/4 fl oz light vegetable oil, e.g. canola
or sunflower oil, plus extra for oiling
300 ml/10 fl oz unsweetened almond
or soya milk
grated zest of 2 lemons
100 ml/3½ fl oz lemon juice
1 tsp vanilla extract
250 g/9 oz plain flour
150 g/5 oz unrefined granulated sugar
1 tsp baking powder
½ tsp bicarbonate of soda
¼ tsp salt
3 tbsp poppy seeds

Preheat the oven to 190°C/375°F/Gas Mark 5. Lightly oil a 450-g/1-lb loaf tin with vegetable oil.

Whisk the milk, vegetable oil, lemon zest, lemon juice and vanilla together.

In another bowl, mix the dry ingredients together.

Pour the wet ingredients into the dry and stir until just combined. Don't over-mix! Pour into the tin and bake for 45–55 minutes, rotating once midway through. Insert a knife or skewer into the cake to test if it is ready – if it comes out clean, it is cooked; if it comes out with batter on it, cook for another 10 minutes.

Index